THE *Hero's* HEART

MELIA KEETON-DIGBY

WOMANCRAFT PUBLISHING

Published by Womancraft Publishing, 2019
www.womancraftpublishing.com

ISBN 978-1-910559-43-7
The Hero's Heart is also available in ebook format: ISBN 978-1-910559-42-0

Cover design, internal illustrations and layout by Lucent Word, www.lucentword.com
Cover art Tache/Shutterstock.com

Womancraft Publishing is committed to sharing powerful new women's voices, through a collaborative publishing process. We are proud to midwife this work, however the story, the experiences and the words are the author's alone. A percentage of Womancraft Publishing profits are invested back into the environment reforesting the tropics (via TreeSisters) and forward into the community: providing books for girls in developing countries, and affordable libraries for red tents and women's groups around the world.

PRAISE FOR
THE HERO'S HEART

Too many mothers feel alone in how to help their sons resist the heavy pressures toxic patriarchy exerts. Melia Keeton-Digby has created a warm, supportive, connected path for moms to take along with our boys. She invites us to step up with courage and use her well-tested, detailed plans for small mother-son circles that meet for a year or more. This book is an awesome gift to feminist moms and boys everywhere. It's a lifeline of hope that can keep boys from losing themselves in the patriarchy of the larger culture. It's the other half of the equation to making our culture fair and supportive to both genders.

Nancy Gruver, founder of the award-winning magazine by and for girls,
New Moon: The Magazine for Girls and Their Dreams

Melia Keeton-Digby, author of The Heroine's Club: A Mother-Daughter Empowerment Circle and founder of The Mother-Daughter Nest, now uses her discerning expertise and intuitive spirituality to examine the crucial relationship between mothers and sons and how that relationship can provide a strong foundation for boys as they grow into men. Let this practical guide be your road map to helping boys navigate the challenges of toxic masculinity through a series of monthly group activities, inspirational quotes, and thoughtful advice on creating and running a "sacred circle" for boys. As Keeton-Digby writes, "Raising our sons is among the most important social imprints we will leave on the world, for they will become the partners, husbands, fathers, friends, lovers, creators, and leaders of tomorrow." Indeed! Timely, relevant, and empowering, this book will make mothers and sons think; it will make them feel; and it will lay the groundwork for connecting heads to hearts in a world where compassion has historically been relegated to the female domain. Parenthood is busy, but this is a project well worth undertaking because the stakes are so high and the rewards so great.

Lori Day, educational psychologist and author of
Her Next Chapter: How Mother-Daughter Book Clubs Can Help Girls Navigate Malicious Media, Risky Relationships, Girl Gossip, and So Much More

In *The Hero's Heart*, Melia Keeton-Digby inspires mothers to create intentional communities, powerful character-shaping opportunities, and much needed rites-of-passage opportunities with their sons. It provides a structure in which moms can enjoy and guide the emotional experience of raising early adolescent boys in our complex world.

Michael Gurian, author of
***The Wonder of Boys and Saving Our Sons*, and co-founder of the Gurian Institute**

I've always thought that the standard narrative – whether the Freudian notion that boys must renounce mother and identify with father on their way to a secure manhood, or the more mytho-poetic notion that only men can initiate boys to manhood – gave short shrift to the power of mothers in shaping boys lives. Mothers can anchor their sons and validate human qualities that may be wrongly thought of as feminine: compassion, caring, resilience, love. As the ones who bear children, they can teach their own children the awesome power and the gorgeous vulnerability of bringing a new life into the world. If they are to flourish as the men they want to be – as friends, fathers, lovers and partners, husbands and colleagues – boys need to know connection and community as much as autonomy. Melia Keeton-Digby's book provides a road map for mothers and sons to remain connected, which enables boys to grow into men who are grounded and ethical.

Michael Kimmel, author of
Guyland: The Perilous World Where Boys Become Men
and *Angry White Men: American Masculinity at the End of an Era*,
Executive Director of the Center for the Study of Men and Masculinities

For Erick and Lucas,

My Sons, My Heroes

Without the honor of loving you, I wouldn't have known.

ACKNOWLEDGEMENTS

The book you are holding in your hands exists thanks to Lucy Pearce and Patrick Treacy of Womancraft Publishing. Lucy and Patrick, you are my publishing family and Womancraft is my home where I feel safe, loved, championed, and understood. For two books in a row, plus all the in-between, you've gone well beyond the call of duty as brilliant editors, passionate publicists, and revolutionary publishers. Thank you for believing in my work and holding the vision with me.

I am grateful to the many authors, researchers, and revolutionaries whose remarkable work and insights I draw on frequently. *The Hero's Heart* stands on the shoulders of giants. Thank you to Adrienne Rich, Ann F. Caron, bell hooks, Beth Rashbaum, Christina Baldwin, Christina Hoff Sommers, Crystal Smith, Deborah David, Eckhart Tolle, Fred Kaeser, Gavin de Becker, Gloria Steinem, Gordon Neufeld, James A. Doyle, Jean Shinoda Bolen, Kate Lombardi, Marshall B. Rosenburg, Michael Gurian, Michael Kimmel, Michael Thompson, Niobe Way, Olga Silverstein, Paul Kivel, Peter A. Levine, Renee Beck, Richard Frankel, Robert Brannon, Ronald F. Levant, Rosalind Wiseman, Rudolf Steiner, Scott Peck, Teresa Barker, and William Pollack.

I grew up sitting at the feet of women in circle and those early experiences created within me an enduring blueprint for how to hold sacred space. Thank you to La Leche League International and La Leche League of South Carolina and Georgia for teaching me the art of circling and community.

Thank you to Baraka Elihu for being foundational in seeding my work as a sacred circle facilitator. Experiencing first-hand the power of your 'Birthing Ourselves into Being' women's circles encouraged me to cultivate my own gifts of leadership and inspired me to apply the medicine of sacred circling to the mother-child relationship. Like cousins from the same lineage, our kinship can no doubt be heard echoing throughout this book.

Thank you to Autumn Weaver, co-creatress of 'Birthing Ourselves into Being.' The gift of sitting alongside you in circle, hearing your heartspeak and absorbing your words, acted as pebbles thrown deep into the waters of my heart, casting powerful ripples that can be, no doubt, felt in this book. I often recall the words you offered that shifted everything for me: *infinitely gentle*.

Thank you to my mother and father, Jim and Sandy, who gave me the one thing any child ever really needs: unconditional love.

I am incredibly grateful to my siblings, Lindsay Jeffcoat and Sean Woods, and their families, for their consistent encouragement and support. Thank you for believing in *The Hero's Heart* (and me!) from the very beginning. Sean, thank you for giving your time, energy, and considerable talent to helping me take this book from a solid *B* to a strong *A+*. The two of you and the inextricable bond we share means the world to me.

To my best friend, Amy. Thank you for the *years* you have fearlessly and fastidiously stood by me. You are my sister and I will always love you.

For the members of the original Hero's Heart circle: Lindsay and John Ross, Mandy and Quentin, Jennie and Wyatt, Kate and Jack, Sandy and Oliver, Beth and Julian, Deena and Noah, Angela and Harper, and Erick. What we have shared together is a reflection of our highest ideals and I will always count our time together in the Nest among the greatest honors of my life. Month after transformational month, *we did this. The Hero's Heart* would literally not exist without you.

To my children: Lucas, Erick, and Della. If all the children in the universe were lined up and I could handpick three to raise, it would be you three. Pop and I are the most grateful parents and our love for you is inestimable. Everything is for you.

To my husband, Rick, the soulmate who makes it all possible. Joining up with you was the best thing I ever did. Ever onward, my beloved.

And finally, gratitude to you, dear reader. You won't find a bigger fan than me. I am your true sister, right here in the middle with you. I am convinced there is nothing we cannot tackle, solve, dream, or create for our children. Thank you for joining me.

FOREWORD

I came of age during the tumultuous sixties and the second wave of feminism. While we usually think of feminism in terms of women's rights, it's really about equal rights and opportunities for *all people.* When it came time for me to have children, I was blessed with two boys and two girls so that my home became the perfect "laboratory" in which to observe the similarities and differences between them.

Feminism taught me to reject pink and blue gender stereotypes – pink was a "boy" color 100 years ago, after all – and I was careful to provide toys that crossed gender lines. My boys played with dolls, often anatomically correct. My girls played with trucks. One of my favorite photos from that time is of my oldest son holding a football while wearing panty hose.

Gender-free toys took care of themselves, largely because of the age distribution of my children. My oldest daughter dressed her two younger brothers in girl clothes when it was important to a story they were acting out. On the flip side, my youngest son and youngest daughter played with GI Joes for hours. I even went so far as to change the gender of characters in stories to suit the listener: my daughter didn't find out that Christopher Robin was a boy until she was a teenager. It was easy to see that my children chose no strict gender roles for themselves and that both my boys and my girls enjoyed all kinds of play – as long as they were exposed to it.

I cried when I read *The Hero's Heart* because it acknowledges something that my home-experiment also demonstrated to me. It is boys who are the most tender and vulnerable. In an article in the *New York Times*, 'The Boys are not All Right,' Michael Ian Black, says:

Too many boys are trapped in the same suffocating, outdated model of masculinity, where manhood is measured in strength, where there is no way to be vulnerable without being emasculated, where manliness is about having power over others. They are trapped, and they don't even have the language to talk about how they feel about being trapped, because the language that exists to discuss the full range of human emotion is still viewed as sensitive and feminine.

Black goes on to suggest that men open themselves to "the rich complexity of manhood" and benefit from "the same conversations girls and women have been having for these past fifty years."

Fortunately, these kinds of conversations were taking place in my community when my children were growing up. Men's groups were starting in my hometown, some of which are still going on today, and in 1990 Robert Bly published his seminal book, *Iron John: A Book About Men* in which he offers a new vision about what it means to be a man and mourns the disappearance of male initiation rites in our culture.

In 1988, Joseph Campbell published *The Power of Myth*, a national bestseller about how ancient stories of the hero's journey continue to bring meaning to our lives. Campbell's earlier book, *The Hero with a Thousand Faces* (1949) was the inspiration for George Lucas' *Star Wars*. I was also influenced by Joseph Chilton Pearce's *Magical Child* (1977), in which he writes eloquently about the importance of play and of young children's bond with nature.

At about this time, I first began hearing of rites of passages for menarche and for teens and created informal and sometimes spontaneous rites of passage for my children. They had the good fortune to participate in a rite of passage retreat called "The Adventure Game Theater."

I had the unique opportunity to raise my children with an awareness of the gender stereotypes of our times. While we encourage our girls to think big and shoot for the moon because we know they may not have equal opportunity, we forget to teach our boys that they too can make choices outside of the cultural norm. If we want an equitable society, we have to give our boys more choices. As Gloria Steinem says, "I'm glad we've begun to raise our daughters more like our sons, but it will never work until we raise our sons more like our daughters."

In Sweden, state school curricula urge pre-school teachers to help counteract traditional gender roles and gender patterns in the hopes of breaking down the norm of stoic, unemotional Swedish masculinity. Swedish teachers avoid referring to their student's gender. Instead of boys and girls, they use friend or call children by name. In fact, Sweden is the first country in history in which a gender-neutral pronoun, *hen*, has been swiftly and successfully absorbed into mainstream culture. According to one peer-reviewed examination of these efforts, Swedish children do not show a strong preference for playmates of the same gender, and are less likely to make assumptions based on gender.

Here are some ways to balance gender at home and in school:

· Encourage both boys and girls to cry.

· Encourage both girls and boys to express their feelings.

· Let children be themselves and follow their own interests.

· Don't make assumptions about a child's preferences based on gender.

· Give children role models of powerful women and compassionate men.

· Offer boys and girls the same choices and opportunities.

· Offer open-ended activities.

· Call out stereotypes.

- Teach both girls and boys to clean, cook and care for themselves.
- Teach both boys and girls to take care of others by modeling empathy to them and to others.
- Share household chores in an egalitarian way.
- Encourage boys to have friendships with girls and girls to have friendships with boys.
- Organize co-ed birthday parties and sports teams.
- Require children to ask before they touch another person's body.
- Teach and model that "no" means "no."
- Speak up when children act inappropriately.
- Model cooperative problem-solving at home.
- Talk to your boy. Talk to him about his feelings. Hug him.
- Don't make the mistake of thinking your son doesn't need you once he grows taller than you.
- Read to your boys as well as your girls.
- Encourage girls and boys to read books about a wide variety of people.
- Speak up when you see teasing, harassment or abuse in public.
- Be careful not to use "girl" as an insult.
- Celebrate boyhood.

So, you ask, how did it go with my sons? Did all those dolls and crying and rites of passage make a difference? Of course they did. One of my sons plays with cars for a living. The other is a martial arts instructor. They both talk easily about their feelings and neither has forgotten how to cry. Plus, my girls are all right too.

With the guidance of *The Hero's Heart*, you can help your son to explore the core values and themes he most needs to cross over the bridge to healthy manhood. You are the bumper rails on that bridge. He may sometimes appear to reject your values as he crosses over, but rest assured, in the end he will embrace whatever your loving environment has taught him.

Peggy O'Mara
Editor and Publisher, Mothering Magazine
Editor and Publisher, peggyomara.com
June 2018

CONTENTS

PART I

It takes courage to grow up and become who you really are.

ee.cummings

INTRODUCTION

> *We who care about the lives of boys and men have an immediate and profound mission, inherent in our position as mothers and fathers, teachers, citizens, and friends. That mission is nothing less than to help each boy develop into a creative spirit, a trustworthy friend, moral leader, and meaningful man. Our mission is nothing less than to protect and nurture the future of humanity.*
> **Michael Gurian,** *The Purpose of Boys*

Do you remember that special moment when you first gazed into your son's eyes and really saw the essence of him? Do you remember when you first felt the sheer miracle of his being? We all have wonderful dreams for our children when we first see them, whether they are born to us, chosen through adoption, or blended through new relationships. I know that you have many gifts in mind that you desperately want to give to your growing son, such as a close relationship with you, self-love, confidence, integrity, the ability to make healthy choices, and a desire to create a positive imprint on the world. This mission probably rooted itself in your mind in that early moment, when you were awash in love and tenderness. Unfortunately, all too often, the complexities of the modern world can impede our progress as we meet life head on with responsibilities, schedules, finances, careers, chores, and the to-do lists that seem to only grow longer with each passing year. Our culture is working against us as we endeavor to raise sons who remain true to themselves while negotiating society's parochial view of masculinity. The dilemma facing modern mothers is to keep an abiding promise to those pure gifts in the face of these multiple challenges. The book you are holding in your hands offers a powerful and accessible path to rediscover those dreams you first had for your beloved son, as well as the structure to explicitly and proactively give the gifts you most wish for him to develop.

What is the Hero's Heart?

The Hero's Heart: A Coming of Age Circle for Boys (And the Mothers Who Love Them) is a revolutionary twelve-month journey for mothers and sons, ages 9–14, to explore the core values and themes our boys need most at this point of their passage to healthy young manhood. Through a set of creative social-emotional lesson plans, complete with thought-provoking discussion questions, inspiring activities, and simple rituals, *The Hero's Heart* offers a practical template to create an intentional community in which your son will thrive, and where you as his mother will find support.

By sharing the Hero's Heart together, your son will learn:

- He is deeply loved and his life has a purpose.

- A strong sense of self, so that he may possess the awareness and courage to more deeply embody the essence of his being.

- To be comfortable with intimacy, authenticity, and vulnerability in relationships with others.

- To recognize, deconstruct, and challenge gender stereotypes and discrimination.

- To develop a real relationship with his own inner guidance system by learning to listen to and trust his intuition.

- The importance of lifelong self-care, including safely navigating alcohol and drugs.

- The influence of mindfulness and gratitude on mental health.

- That self-advocating is both his right and his responsibility.

- To think for himself, speak his truth, and stand strong in the face of negative peer pressure.

- The essentials of conflict resolution and the foundations of nonviolent, assertive communication.

- An emotional vocabulary and the ability to recognize, tolerate, express, and communicate all feelings in productive ways.

- To honor and understand the physical and emotional changes both boys and girls experience as they enter puberty.

- Respect and reverence for his own body and for women's bodies, through developmentally appropriate discussions on masturbation, sex, pornography, body sovereignty, and consent.

- To follow his natural gifts and passions to find his place in the world through purpose-driven service.

- That the journey to manhood is sacred, and that he has a loving community invested in guiding and supporting him along the way.

The really great news is that this program is completely doable, even for the busiest of mothers! Whether you are hoping to start a Hero's Heart mother-son circle in your community, planning to share it with a few other close mother/son pairs, or even hoping to simply do it alone with your son, I will lay out a clear, easy-to-use template for building your own Hero's Heart circle and this book will take you every step of the way through implementing the curriculum for a year of life-changing transformation for your boy.

How *The Hero's Heart* Came To Be

My calling to serve the current and future generations of young men was actually born out of my work with girls. I have three children and at the time of this writing, Lucas is eighteen, Erick is thirteen, and Della is nine. As my youngest child and only daughter moved through young girlhood, I recognized a staggering divide between how the world was experienced by girls, and how I knew it needed to be. Particularly, I was struck by the outright lack of women's history and positive female role models being offered in schools and society in general, and I wanted my daughter to grow up knowing that she and her sisters had far more to offer the world than just a pretty appearance. I wanted my daughter to know the full range of who she might become, and so I created the Heroines Club, which is based on the studying and sharing of women's history with our daughters. This mother-daughter circle explores key issues, such as believing in one's dreams, advocating for one's self, speaking one's truth, the importance of challenging gender stereotypes and discrimination, fostering a positive body image, and resiliency. The Heroines Club has been a tremendous success in my community, and the curriculum was collected into a book so that other mothers and daughters around the world could reap the same benefits. It was actually a photograph, taken at the launch party of *The Heroines Club: a mother-daughter empowerment circle* (Womancraft Publishing, 2016), that awoke in me the drive to create a program that would serve our sons in the same way that the Heroines Club serves our daughters.

Within days after the truly amazing launch of my first book, the buzz of celebration was somewhat interrupted by a new reflection. I found myself walking into work at my local high school, where I serve as a speech-language pathologist, with my subconscious ruminating on this picture of my middle child, Erick, and me. As I walked, I replayed a conversation in my head that I had experienced many times before since I was first called to create the Heroines Club. Along with great enthusiasm and gratitude from the mothers of my community, I was also frequently asked the question:

What about our sons?

I had become unsatisfied with my usual response to this question:
"I'm all for our sons! I was a mother to my sons for years before I had a daughter. I am deeply devoted to raising empowered, nurtured, emotionally expressive, verbal, nonviolent

sons! It's just not what I am called to do for the community. Besides, isn't that the father's place? Shouldn't a father start something? Please do! I'll sign my boys right up! And anyway, the whole world is the "Heroes Club"!

And just like that, I heard my inner voice gently whisper back to me:

"Yeah, but *Erick doesn't know that.*"

I stopped dead in my tracks. I slipped my bag from my shoulder to the ground, and looked up into the morning sky as I heard the words echo in my heart.

Erick doesn't know that.

It was one of those "aha moments" in life. In that moment, I realized I was assuming that our boys had the maturity to interpret the oppressive history of patriarchy and understand what I was trying to do with *The Heroines Club*. Yet, our sons are not the oppressors; they too are victims of patriarchy! There are many patriarchal structures yet to be dismantled. If we are to truly change the world, must not we bring our sons equally into this conversation?

This wholly unexpected moment of divine insight left me with one big question:

Am I leaving our sons behind to the toxic culture I have fought so hard against for our daughters?

Reflecting more, I knew that the past year had been hard for Erick, and at times, hard for me as his mother. Fourth grade presented many new challenges and I had privately supported Erick as he wrestled with growing up. I realized the themes that we had worked through were the same as those that I was addressing every month with mothers and daughters at Heroines Club (speaking our truth, failure and resiliency, self-advocating, unconditional love, intuition, courage, self-confidence, expressing feelings, etc.). With more than a little sadness, I thought of how Erick would have benefited from a dedicated discussion of these topics in a safe and sacred community. But could a similar arrangement really work? Sons and mothers circling together? It seems incredibly foolish to me now, but I really got stuck here for a few days, questioning whether a circle of mothers could lead their boys into young manhood.

I dove into deep contemplation and read some really important books (check out the recommended resources at the end of this book for a complete list) and the answer became clear: it was the patriarchy itself convincing me that only a man could effectively mentor a boy, or that boys might be "too wild" to share in the practice of sacred circling, or that boys might not enjoy or know how to talk about feelings or share crafts, ritual, and ceremony in the way girls do. I was shocked and embarrassed at the limiting beliefs that I had unconsciously harbored, despite having such close and deep relationships with my own sons.

Around the same time as these ruminations, the daily news was filled with heartbreaking stories of the displacement of over sixty-five million refugees from around the world because of persecution, war, violence, and human rights violations. One evening before going to sleep, I read the story of a real-life heroine that deeply touched my heart. Yusra Mardini was a fifteen-year-old girl whose home in Syria had been destroyed in a civil war. In the face of extreme violence and under the threat of death, she and her sister were compelled to attempt fleeing their homeland. In August, 2015, Yusra and her sister Sarah crammed themselves into a tiny, overcrowded dinghy filled with too many other men, women, and children, and set out on the Mediterranean Sea. At some point on their treacherous escape, the boat's motor faltered and the vessel began to take on water. The passengers were hysterical, sure that since many did not know how to swim, they would drown. Yusra, a strong swimmer, dove out of the boat and into the cold ocean water to push the boat for over three hours until reaching land and relative safety. The report I read that evening ended with the good news that for the first time in Olympic history, a team of refugees (named the Refugee Olympic Team) would be competing in the Summer Olympics, and Yusra had been officially named to swim for the team!

My heart must have resonated with this story on a metaphorical level, for that night, I had a dream. I was in the water, pushing a broken-down boat full of boys to safety, with my own beloved son leaning over the edge, encouraging me onward. When I awoke the next morning, I knew what I had to do. I answered the call to serve our sons with a big, resounding "yes, and thank you," and then I got to work.

Boots on the Ground

In creating the Hero's Heart circle for my son and my community, I examined the most influential books on boys of our time and I found that they all shared a common paradigm: to heal, men and boys must learn to feel again. However, most of the current books on the market stop too soon. What is missing, and what *The Hero's Heart* seeks to address, is a strategy to free our sons from the rigid script of "appropriate maleness" which is the root cause of this paucity of emotional vocabulary in boys today. *The Hero's Heart* takes the best theory from the leaders in the field of boyhood and male psychology, and applies it to doable action. Born from the efforts of an intense research process, coupled with my firsthand knowledge of adolescent boys garnered through my fifteen-plus years as an educator in the public school system, and finally, wrapped in my mother-love for my own two sons, *The Hero's Heart* is boots-on-the-ground activism on behalf of our boys. This book and the curriculum within is an attempt to respond explicitly and proactively to the needs and the capacities of our young boys and to their right to a healthy, meaningful transition into young manhood.

A Place for Our Boys

The Hero's Heart seeks to be one of the first socially sanctioned opportunities for boys to create a sense of self that is distinct from sexist definitions. Today's feminist movement has rightfully worked to extend this freedom to our daughters and as a culture, "Girl Power" is on the forefront of our evolved social consciousness. For women and girls, the collective mainstream has begun to shift, and as a society, we are becoming more aware of damaging and limiting gender stereotypes as applied to the female half of the population. But what about our sons? Our boys need empowerment just as much as our girls. They too need a safe place to air their worries, to find their voices, and to feel the freedom to be who they truly are, gender stereotypes be damned. The time is right to raise our collective awareness about the development of healthy masculinity. Although more awareness exists about the negative aspects of stereotypes regarding girls, the patterns around boys are equally destructive unless we meet them directly. Our daughters may seem more vulnerable to us, but as I will discuss in the chapter *Boyhood Today: Going Off-Script*, our sons are too! Furthermore, our daughters will not be fully free to reach their complete potential if their male counterparts are left behind. As bell hooks writes in *The Will to Change: Men, Masculinity, and Love*, "We cannot journey far if boys are left behind. They wield too much power to be simply ignored or forgotten." She goes on to say, "those of us who love men do not want to continue our journey without them. We need them beside us because we love them." I firmly believe that gender equality is not a zero-sum game. We need our heroines, and we need our heroes too.

Who This Book Was Written For

Adolescence is unlike any other period in life. Above all, this is a time of deep transformation. The boys for whom this book is written are in the midst of a tumultuous transition between two stages of development – boyhood and early young manhood. Our adolescent sons are eager to become heroes in our eyes, and in the eyes of the world. This circle experience will illuminate for our sons what it truly means to be a hero, far beyond the hyper-masculine tropes that today's pop culture offers. The ultimate goal of *The Hero's Heart* is to assist mothers during this pivotal phase to nurture their boys' inner qualities – the hero's heart – so that those boys will retain and develop their whole selves as they navigate the maze of issues that boys in our culture must face.

The Hero's Heart focuses primarily on sons in the 9-14 age group, while also providing lessons and insights that can be immediately applied throughout a boy's life, regardless of his age. If you are mothering a son, then this book is for you.

This book is also a resource for a variety of other adults who work with boys – fathers, teachers, school administrators, psychologists, social workers, and other mentors. For example, a teacher reading this book might recognize the way he or she inadvertently reinforces gender stereotypes in the classroom, or receive a new insight into how to facilitate positive communication among male students. It is my hope that this book will reach as many adults as possible who share the mission of helping all boys reach their full potential.

How to Use This Book

In Part I, I examine the needs of boys today and highlight the ways in which *The Hero's Heart* directly meets those needs. I affirm mothers' ability (and responsibility) to stay connected with their sons as they journey into and through adolescence, as well as address the role of fathers in this program. Finally, I explain in detail what is meant by the term 'sacred circle' and how the key elements of this practice are at the root of what makes this program so nourishing and transformative for sons and mothers alike. This section of the book is a rally call that will leave you feeling impassioned and inspired to, as hero Mahatma Gandhi taught us, "be the change you wish to see in the world."

In Part II, I share everything you need to set up your own Hero's Heart circle experience for your son. I cover concerns such as whom to invite, where to meet, what age range to include, and what is an ideal circle size. I cover important ways to keep your circle healthy and strong, such as reviewing the agreements at every circle, periodic "health of the circle" check-ins, dealing with conflict between members, and maintaining connection between circle gatherings. Finally, Part II ends with clear and comprehensive instructions for how to implement *The Hero's Heart* curriculum. Here the sequence of circle events is delineated, followed by a detailed explanation of how to best implement each section, with helpful advice and even direct scripts that can be taken and used. This section of the book will answer all of your questions and leave you feeling ready and able to give the magic of *The Hero's Heart* to your son.

Part III is a complete and detailed one-year curriculum. Here you will find fourteen complete circle templates: an initial mothers-only intention-setting circle, the twelve monthly circles, and the closing circle and powerful rite of passage ceremony.

We Are In This Together

The Hero's Heart circle I created for my son and for my community has surpassed even my loftiest hopes. Our local group has been changing the trajectory of these young men's lives forever. In circle, the wisdom and openness that emerges from the boys is breathtaking. At the end of each monthly gathering, we mothers privately look at each other wide-eyed as if to say, "Wow! What we are doing here is revolutionary!"

Heroine Dr. Maya Angelou taught us, "When you learn, teach. When you get, give." I knew that I had a moral imperative to write this book so that you too might reap the same benefits by which my community has been blessed.

The last line I wrote in my book, *The Heroines Club*, was, "Our daughters need us and we are the ones we have been waiting for." I am now saying our sons need us too, and perhaps even more so we are the ones we have been waiting for. Raising our sons is among the most important social imprints we will leave on the world, for they will become the partners, husbands, fathers, friends, lovers, creators, and leaders of tomorrow. Dear mothers, we know the boat carrying our boys is sinking. Now it is time for us to jump in and swim.

We are in this together.

Love, *Melia*

BOYHOOD TODAY:
GOING OFF-SCRIPT

> *The first act of violence that patriarchy demands of males is [...] that they engage in acts of psychic self-mutilation, that they kill off the emotional parts of themselves. If an individual is not successful in emotionally crippling himself, he can count on patriarchal men to enact rituals of power that will assault his self-esteem.*
>
> **bell hooks**

When we come into this world, we are born within a system that delivers us a pre-determined 'script' to follow based on our sex. Those of us with the female phenotype are expected to play one character (femininity), while those with the male phenotype are told to play another (masculinity). We are then socialized in myriad ways to embody this script, which essentially governs our lives from day one. The title of this system – this script – is *patriarchy*.

What is Patriarchy?

Patriarchy is an unjust political-social system in which males hold primary power and predominate in all the major institutions of society, including government and roles of political leadership, religion and moral authority, education, the economy and control of property, the military, and the media. For at least the last few millennia, every country in the world has been patriarchal.

Patriarchy is as much a collective mindset as it is a concrete set of structures and institutions. The human behaviors that support patriarchy are related to the assumptions we carry about people based on their gender, even if we don't necessarily believe that one sex is superior to the other. Patriarchy is perpetuated and sustained (by both men and women) through these gender role assumptions, much like characters in a play.

Although men are, as a class, the group seemingly advantaged by patriarchy, this system is oppressive to all people because it demands both sexes to relinquish their rights to authenticity and wholeness. Boys and girls become alienated from significant parts of themselves in their socialization along gender lines. For boys, our culture tries to raise them to carry a tough, stoic suit of armor, and the outcomes can be deadly.

According to recent statistics:

- Suicide is the second leading cause of death for men under thirty-five. Men are four times more likely than women to die from suicide. Although teen girls are more likely than teen boys to attempt suicide, the boys are more likely to actually complete a suicide attempt. They are less likely to allow for intervention, and they are less likely to use a suicide attempt as a "call for help".

- Substance abuse is a predominantly male problem, occurring at a relative rate of 3 to 1 compared to females.

- Men are significantly less likely to seek mental health services in response to a mental health problem in comparison with women.

- In high school, boy athletes are much more likely than girl athletes to not report symptoms of a concussion for fear of seeming weak.

- Men commit 86% of violent crime and are twice as likely to be victims of violent crimes.

- Men comprise 95% of the U.S. prison population.

- The average lifespan for men in the U.S. is five years shorter than for women, and about seven years shorter for men than women worldwide.

Thankfully, just like a play relies on its characters to move the plot forward, so the patriarchy relies on us to keep it operating. Patriarchy and gender roles are just social constructs, dependent on prevailing norms and prone to evolution. This means that gender roles – the rights, responsibilities, opportunities, and behaviors assigned to males and females – are set by society, and *we are society!* Patriarchy is not some monolithic leviathan outside of us. We are the patriarchy. Each of us is a powerful member of the society in which we live, and as the old saying goes, "the personal is political." Changing our world depends not only on voting, protesting, and supporting progressive government policies. Our power also lies in making changes in our own lives, in our own homes, and in our own communities. The revolutionary path to a more egalitarian world requires that we reveal, analyze, and reconstruct the patriarchy's restrictive gender scripts – for both girls and boys.

Recent societal progress related to raising girls can serve as a springboard to improving the situation for our boys. For more than thirty years, girls have been increasingly encouraged to "go off-script" in many ways and embrace traits that were once considered traditionally masculine, such as competing athletically, academically, and professionally, developing their own strong voices, demonstrating leadership, and being assertive. For many of us, once we perceived the damaging effects of the patriarchal structures on our daughters, we strove to change the way we raised them. Despite many persistent and ongoing challenges, the world is a very different place than it used to be for Western females. Many of us are now beginning to look at boyhood in the same critical way. We know that we should be encouraging *all* of our children to be strong and brave leaders, as well as to be kind and communicative nurturers. Both our girls and our boys deserve to experience and share their full humanity. Furthermore, these traits are not mutually exclusive; the best leaders are nurturers who are brave and kind, strong and communicative. Before we dive into *The Hero's Heart* curriculum in Parts II and III, we will first explore why a new paradigm is critically needed for our sons.

Let's first take a closer look at the masculine 'script' for boys and what makes it so damaging. In the next chapter, we will explore how *The Hero's Heart* works to shift the paradigm, allowing our boys' sense of self to remain fully intact.

Revealing and Analyzing the Masculine Script

Research on boys, men, and masculinity has flourished over the last two decades and has documented a host of negative outcomes for those who adhere to the traditional Western masculinity norms. Dr. Ronald F. Levant is one of the world's leading authorities on the psychology of men and masculinity. Through his pioneering research, he identified seven prescriptive norms and stereotypes for boys and men in a patriarchy. They are: avoidance of all things feminine, restricting the expression of emotions, achievement and status as the top priority, self-reliance through independence, focus on toughness and aggression, homophobia, and nonrelational and objectifying attitudes toward sexuality. Let's consider the implications of each of these main mandates of manhood and the psychic price our boys pay.

The Seven Main Stereotypes for Boys and Men

1. AVOID BEING FEMININE

What is a boy? *Not* a girl. This is perhaps the most traumatizing and dangerous injunction thrust upon men and boys. James A. Doyle, author of *The Male Experience*, explains that the first maxim of the male script is "don't be like a girl." Boys are expected to reject any and all signs of the innate human qualities that patriarchy labels "feminine," such as empathy, sensitivity, and the desire to nurture. They are punished for showing vulnerability and pressured to demean feminine qualities as a way of boosting their masculine image. Doyle believes this avoidance of all things "feminine" is the origin of a deep splintering in a boy's core self. It is also the foundation of misogyny because in adopting these directives and rejecting the "feminine" parts of themselves, boys internalize that women and girls are "unequal, bad, and inferior." This toxic maxim is at the root of the other six male stereotypes.

2. RESTRICT EMOTIONS

From a very early age, boys are bombarded with the message – from outside and sometimes even inside the home – to keep their emotions in check and to "act like a man." *Keep a stiff upper lip. Suck it up. Play through pain.* Be stoic and stable. Never show any weakness. Never whimper, complain, or grieve openly. Most of all, never, ever cry. Every day, boys receive one message about how to deal with emotions, and that message is: *don't*.

In *Raising Cain: Protecting the Emotional Life of Boys*, the authors Dan Kindlon and Michael Thompson argue that boys in our culture are steadily directed away from their emotional lives and toward behaviors such as stoicism and silence. Even though they experience all the normal human feelings (love, excitement, joy, affection, grief, sorrow, fear, confusion, anger, insecurity, etc.), most are taught to hide all feelings except anger so as to appear tough and in control. While girls in our culture are socialized to believe that happiness is the singular emotion they may express and still be loved, boys are taught that anger is the only emotion they may express and still be respected. Because of this, many boys lack the ability to read and understand their own emotions and the emotions of others – a big problem for relationships!

Our culture tries to convince us that girls are hyper-emotional and boys are hypo-emotional, as if this dichotomy was some biological maxim. This notion is contrary, however, to the available evidence; all humans have the same emotional center in the brain, the amygdala. All humans experience a complex tapestry of feelings! And as we know, suppressed feelings do not disappear, but rather they manifest in other ways such as substance abuse, poor school performance, aggressive behavior, extreme risk taking, perfectionism, relationship and intimacy problems, depression, anxiety, panic, and physical ailments.

3. MAKE ACHIEVEMENT THE TOP PRIORITY

Achieving status, power, and domination is woven into stereotypical masculinity. In a patriarchal culture, males are not allowed simply to be who they are and to glory in their unique identities; their value is always determined by their vocation. Men, as individuals, are under tremendous pressure to become a financial success and as a result, their very identity and self-esteem becomes intertwined with their occupational success.

4. EXHIBIT SELF-RELIANCE THROUGH COMPLETE INDEPENDENCE

Patriarchal mores insist that boys must substantiate their manhood by idealizing aloneness and disconnection. This ideal of rugged individualism and the eschewing of any signs of dependency leaves boys and men socially disconnected and isolated, increasing their risk for depression, suicide, premature death, alcohol and substance abuse, and a plethora of other mental and physical health problems. One research study even found that social isolation can be as much of a long-term risk factor to health as smoking. Dr. Vivek Murthy, the Surgeon General of the United States, has said many times in recent years that the most prevalent health issue in the country is not cancer or heart disease or obesity. It is isolation.

This social edict has a particularly detrimental effect on the mother-son relationship. This subject will be discussed in depth in the chapter *Mothers and Sons, Together*. Here though, it is important to note that mother-love remains taboo among most teenage boys with the contemptible "mama's boy" remaining the prevailing mother-son archetype in our culture. Therefore, beginning around age nine, ten, or eleven, a boy following the patriarchal script for masculinity will push his feelings for his mother underground, and unfortunately, some well-intentioned mothers do the same. This loss cuts to the deepest part of a boy, isolating him from a principal source of affection and belonging.

Boys are not only restricted from being close with or expressing feelings toward their mother, boys also receive a clear message that they should not be too close with another boy. Within their friendships with other boys, social norms are extremely limiting. Observe any group of boys together in a social setting and you will notice that they swagger, they heckle, they joke, but they do not share feelings. They do not share their authentic selves. They relate in a scripted, limited way, ever-careful to remain within the emotional boundaries set by patriarchal thinking about masculinity. Boys experience much pressure to cut off their emotional intimacy with their male friends and so they constantly test each other and jockey for position, looking for any signs of vulnerability. Reacting to peer pressure with its homophobic underpinnings leads boys to interact in three monolithic ways: compete, control, or criticize.

5. INGRAIN HOMOPHOBIA

The pervasive level of homophobia in middle schools and high schools is staggering. "That's so gay!" is one of the common put-downs boys use to shame one another back on script by associating them with homosexuality and femininity.

By a strict definition, homophobia is the hatred and irrational fear of gay men and women. But the real issue goes much deeper than that. Homophobia and its associated acts relate to a deep-seated fear that one might not be a "real man" himself and so he must constantly assert his masculinity and, once again, take great pains to repress parts of himself.

Homophobia obviously hurts those of our sons who are, or will be, gay, but it also impacts all boys regardless of their sexual orientation because of the need to be constantly vigilant and self-monitoring so as not to "lose your manhood."

6. ACT TOUGH AND AGGRESSIVE

Be the first to challenge. Don't ever show that you are scared. Try to make other boys afraid of you first. Fight and win. From an early age, boys are taught to be tough and physical, and that violence is an acceptable response to emotional upset. The most popular male role models are idealized for being strong, aggressive athletes and superheroes. War heroes are put on pedestals and gain fame and infamy through violent actions. Seemingly every male icon – every "hero" – is pictured as violent, aggressive, and uber-muscular, leaving boys feeling that they too must be physically big, very strong, and possess the ability to use violence to gain power.

However, boys are not born tough. They learn to act tough to withstand the brutal masculine system that uses rejection, bullying, terror, and violence to keep boys and men "on script."

7. OBJECTIFY WOMEN AND EXERCISE A NON-RELATIONAL ATTITUDE TOWARD SEX

Too many boys learn at an early age to view women as prizes to be won, rather than as complex people with personalities, talents, intelligences, morals, feelings, wants, and needs of their own.

Objectifying women dehumanizes them, providing a false justification to act toward them with disregard, and even violence.

Sexuality is a significant part of every boy's psychosocial development, but truthfully, children today learn more about sex from mass media and pornography than from any other source. Much of what children are learning conforms to outmoded patriarchal scripts about the sexual nature of men and women. The early influence of these false and toxic scripts about sex shapes boys' entire life experience toward sexuality.

Reconstructing Masculinity: Going Off-Script

> ❝ *We, with love, shall force our brothers to see themselves as they are, to cease fleeing from reality and begin to change it.*
> **James Baldwin, *The Fire Next Time***

The crisis facing our boys today is not masculinity, rather it is toxic patriarchal hyper-masculinity. In many ways, our boys are constantly clashing within themselves between who they really are and who they are expected to be. The stress of guarding and protecting a false self creates a deep wound in the male psyche. Even boys fortunate enough to live in a home that rebukes the patriarchal norms face the stress of living a double life at school and in the community.

We who love boys strive to separate and retain the valuable aspects of traditional masculinity that deserve to be honored (such as leading, building, and protecting) from those that are obsolete or dysfunctional (such as stoicism, aggression, and isolation), while also giving our boys the freedom and encouragement to exercise their innate human qualities traditionally considered "feminine" (such as emotional awareness, nurturing, and interconnection). We seek to create a new definition of masculinity that is broad and inclusive, and thereby reconstruct the script for our boys – or better yet, we seek to encourage boys to follow their own paths and truest selves and write their own scripts.

To reject the harmful code of patriarchal hyper-masculinity is no easy task for men of any age. Most boys genuinely fear going 'off-script.' We must recognize that we are asking our boys to work toward shifting the paradigm within the paradigm itself. This takes courage and heroism. And it also takes support.

That's where the Hero's Heart comes in.

WHAT OUR SONS NEED MOST: THE GIFTS OF THE HERO'S HEART

> *To truly protect and honor the emotional lives of boys we must challenge patriarchal culture. And until that culture changes, we must create the subcultures, the sanctuaries where boys can learn to be who they are uniquely, without being forced to conform to patriarchal masculine visions. To love boys rightly, we must value their inner lives enough to construct worlds, both private and public, where their right to wholeness can be consistently celebrated and affirmed, where their need to love and be loved can be fulfilled.*
> **bell hooks, *The Will to Change: Men, Masculinity, and Love***

By reading this book, you are joining arms with a global community of mothers who witness the crisis looming in the hearts of boys and are taking action on their behalf.

I recognize that the causes of the problems our boys face are complex and varied, and so too are the possible solutions. In addition to the sexism patriarchy prescribes, issues such as racism, classism, heterosexism, poverty, lack of healthcare, and lack of education are all issues with which we must contend. *The Hero's Heart* is not a panacea, but it is a step in the right direction, and most importantly, it is a step we *all* can take.

The Hero's Heart circles I facilitate are comprised of mothers from all walks of life, with a diversity of religion, belief systems, socio-economic status, and backgrounds. We each have different skills, attitudes, and experiences. What unites us is our vision for our sons and our desire to fortify their early-adolescent identities by providing, as hooks put it, "a sanctuary where boys can learn to be who they are uniquely, without being forced to conform to patriarchal masculine visions." We know that by sharing the gifts of the Hero's Heart with our sons, a firm and healthy foundation is being laid for their teen years and beyond.

In Part II and Part III, I will open the door and invite you into our circle, hopefully removing any intimidating mystique or lingering misconceptions about the Hero's Heart. What I most hope you will hear in my words is that I am an everyday woman and mother much like yourself; you too can share the gifts of the Hero's Heart with your son. As mothers raising sons, we have the power to change the trajectory of not only our own sons' lives, but also of the culture at large.

Before we go further, it is helpful to illuminate and consider the gifts of the Hero's Heart. Fully understanding the core intentions of this experience will guide you as you create your own unique version, and will further inspire you to see your efforts through to completion for your community.

By sharing the Hero's Heart with your son, you are giving him:

The Gift of Quality Time

> " *I really appreciate how by participating in the Hero's Heart circle, I am guaranteed to have a monthly date alone with my son! With three children and a full-time job, I know all too well how challenging it can be to actually make meaningful time alone with each child happen. By participating in this circle, it is on my calendar and we are accountable. I feel as excited about and rejuvenated by our circle as my son! Some of our best conversations have happened in the car on the drive home from Hero's Heart. I'm so grateful for it!*
> **Lindsay, Hero's Heart mother**

Quality time is time devoted to being with your son together, offering your whole-hearted attention and engaging in activities you both enjoy, in order to strengthen the relationship. Many events happen throughout our sons' lives that need discussion and processing, and by spending regular quality time with our sons, we give them the comfort level and a recurring opportunity to share these things with us. Your son needs to spend meaningful time with you, individually. In families with more than one child in the home, consciously creating this dedicated time is especially important.

One of the greatest gifts of sharing the Hero's Heart with your son is the built-in structure and nourishing accountability that comes with this fun, monthly-meeting circle. Life can be busy and much time and effort is required from us mothers to maintain the everyday demands of raising our children. Please know that the time you set aside with your son for the Hero's Heart is not just another item on your to-do list (we have enough already!), but rather it is an investment. The focused time and energy spent connecting and having fun together actually makes mothering our sons easier, as all aspects of parenting flow much more smoothly when the relationship is healthy and strong.

The Gift of Sacred Space to Reconnect with Himself

> *I love my Hero's Heart circle because it allows me to express things that I wouldn't normally. A lot of kids don't like to express themselves at school because it makes them feel uncool. They are afraid that if they sound different, people will view them as an outsider. Even though we all feel the same way on the inside, we keep a lot of these things hidden away and don't really talk about them. Hero's Heart gives me a chance to talk about these things.*
> **Oliver, age 13**

So much happens and shifts quickly in an adolescent's world and the storms of growing up can weather a boy's heart. By gathering in circle each month, our boys not only connect with us, but also with themselves. Circle offers them an opportunity to pause, step away from their everyday routine and pressures, see to their hearts, and check-in with *themselves*.

When I was a child and my family visited the Atlantic Ocean on vacation, my father would tie his shoes to the top of our beach umbrella so that when our playing gradually pulled us along the shore, my young siblings and I could easily spot our "home base" among the sea of seemingly identical beach equipment. Like children playing in the ocean, adolescents readily drift off and away – from us, from their own values and ideals, from who they really are – without ever realizing the presence or power of life's many undercurrents. Circle prompts our boys to look up from their lives for a moment, to assess where they are and how things are going, and if they have drifted, to return to the "home base" of their hearts before they've gone too far.

The Gift of Authenticity

> *The Hero's Heart means a lot to me. It is so much fun getting together with everyone each month and discussing a different topic. It has been a safe place to speak the truth and tell what I am thinking about.*
> **Quentin, age 11**

Rarely do boys have an ample opportunity of the space and time to speak their truth and be fully heard without interruption, feedback, advice, or judgement. Most boys are taught that they should only show their strong, confident side and that the countenance they must show the world should *always* be one of perfection, strength, and control. Time, care, and great intention are required to create the environment where boys sense emotional safety enough to remove their masks and relax their defensive posture. You will be surprised at how quickly they can begin to talk earnestly. In circle, boys learn that they will not lose respect when they talk about their problems, and that sharing their vulnerabilities helps them feel close to others and helps others feel close to them. They learn they can safely share their authentic selves.

The Gift of Close Interpersonal Relationships

> *Hero's Heart has really given my son and me an opportunity to bond in such a thoughtful and intelligent way. I love the conversations he has with me now, the trust he has to talk to me about things that he might have felt were too personal or embarrassing before. That's priceless!*
>
> **Angela, Hero's Heart mom**

Circle nurtures close bonds through the modeling of close mother-son relationships among the boys. Socially, adolescent boys feel tremendous pressure to hide the warm feelings they have for their mothers from their peers, but at the Hero's Heart, positive and tender mother-son interactions are the norm.

Additionally, boys learn how to initiate and maintain deep and rich friendships with other boys without the need to dominate.

The Gift of Communication Skills

> *I love how all the boys speak from their hearts. Now, when my son and I discuss topics and issues at home, I notice he seems to be able to communicate from a deeper level of understanding.*
>
> **Deena, Hero's Heart mom**

One of the myths about boys is that they don't talk; expressive language is considered a "girl thing." The reality is, according to William Pollack, author and professor of psychology at Harvard Medical School, boys possess the same vocabulary and a rich tapestry of feelings just as girls do, but they are suppressed from speaking because they are shamed out of the capacity they have. When boys are provided with an encouraging, positive environment, the words start to come.

Participating in the Hero's Heart with your son provides a prime opportunity to counteract this cultural stereotype of reticence and to engage in meaningful conversation together with a circle of other mothers and sons. Despite the societal message about boys' limited communication skills, boys participating in the Hero's Heart will surprise you with their natural emotional expressivity.

Each month in circle offers supported opportunities for substantive and meaningful conversations. Month 6 ("*I Think for Myself and Speak My Truth*") and Month 7 ("*I Am a Peacebuilder*") offer explicit guidance in the areas of active listening, using "I" statements, direct and nonviolent communication, and setting healthy boundaries and firm limits.

The impact of these communicative experiences and practice opportunities cannot be overstated. Effective communication is a life-skill at the root of all personal and professional success. Learning to communicate openly, clearly, and directly is integral to being the heroes of our own lives.

The Gift of Emotional Intelligence

> *If we teach our sons to honor and value their emotional lives, if we can give boys an emotional vocabulary and the encouragement to use it, they will unclench their hearts.*
> **William Pollack, *Real Boys***

In circle each month, we give boys the permission to have a full internal life and the encouragement to express the complete range of their emotions with words. In Month 4 ("*I Express All My Feelings in Healthy Ways*"), we explore the range of feelings humans experience and expand their ability to express themselves in ways beyond anger and aggression. They receive direct practice articulating their feelings, and by witnessing other boys and mothers sharing in circle, they increase their emotional connectedness and develop empathy and compassion.

The Hero's Heart teaches our boys to express what they feel with words and healthy actions. Helping our sons break through the patriarchal code of male silence early in life is one of the greatest gifts we can bestow, for it will have a lifelong impact on how they care for themselves and relate with others.

The Gift of a Healthy Self-Concept

> ❝ *The strongest lesson I can teach my son is the same lesson I teach my daughter: how to be who he wishes to be for himself.*
> **Audre Lorde**

One of the central milestones of adolescence is the development of an identity (the sense of who they are as individuals and as members of social groups). Identity forms the basis of self-esteem (confidence in one's worth), and how our sons assess themselves will impact the choices they make and how well they care for themselves.

Through sharing *The Hero's Heart* curriculum, your son will develop a solid personal foundation of self-knowledge, self-confidence, and self-respect. He will learn to love and accept himself as he is, while knowing that he can improve and develop any aspect of himself that he chooses. He will also learn that as the hero of his own life, he is primarily responsible for his own physical, mental, emotional, and spiritual self-care.

The Gift of Values

> ❝ *My greatest hope for my son is that he will be true to himself and responsible to his community, both large and small. Participating in the Hero's Heart has provided opportunities for us to explore the values that will make this possible.*
> **Beth, Hero's Heart mom**

The Hero's Heart nurtures the internal qualities that build character and teaches boys what it really means to be a hero. Each month, we sharpen their ability to reflect thoughtfully on the world around them and within. In Month 1 ("*I Have the Heart of a Hero*"), we reframe strength, courage, and heroism. Boys learn that courage can manifest in myriad ways and that rather than defining strength as "power over," true strength is one's capacity to be responsible for self and others. In Month 12 ("*I Am Changing the World*"), our sons learn about their responsibilities to: serve their community, protect the natural world, develop their leadership abilities, and thoughtfully analyze the moral implications of their actions.

The Gift of Information

> *Tonight's topic ("I Honor My Changing Body") taught me so much! It's like school, except way better because we talk about the things I'm actually thinking about. I'm not sitting around wondering 'Who was Saddam Hussein?' but I am wondering about what's gonna happen to my body during puberty!*
> **Wyatt, 12, reflecting after circle**

Our boys desperately want to discuss and understand sexuality (even if they act as if they don't), but the opportunity is rare to explicitly examine and discuss the topic in a safe setting that is guided, inclusive, and free of taboo. *The Hero's Heart* approach to sexuality education is based on the conviction that knowledge is empowering. When it comes to an area of life as important and potentially dangerous as sexuality, our sons need accurate and complete information. Mothers (and fathers) need to be the primary source of their sons' sexuality education, and Month 10 ("*I Honor My Changing Body*") and Month 11 ("*Sex is Sacred*") support these efforts.

I know talking about bodies, sexual abuse, masturbation, sexual behaviors, pornography, condoms, and consent can feel scary and intimidating, but we must engage these topics if our children are to safely grow into healthy adults. Research shows that by having the meaningful conversations with your son about sex and sexuality as outlined in Months 10 and 11 of this book, it becomes more likely that he will postpone intercourse until adulthood, avoid impregnating someone in adolescence or contracting a sexually transmitted disease, avoid sexually abusive relationships, and develop a healthy attitude toward sexuality.

The Gift of Purpose and Meaning

> *I appreciate that with Hero's Heart, my son hears about very serious topics in a reverent way. I love that the idea of one's life purpose has been planted in his heart as something to really think about and know.*
> **Mandy, Hero's Heart mom**

Boys need to hear that their hearts matter, that they do not have to do or perform or prove their value and worth, and that they have an important place in this world. By providing a dedicated space to explore the depths of themselves and the world around them, the Hero's

Heart anchors in our boys an inner knowing that they are part of something greater than themselves and that their lives have purpose and meaning.

The Gift of Community

> " *I am so grateful for the Hero's Heart! For me, the most profound part is being able to revisit the words of the other boys and moms in circle with my son… it feels more like community wisdom rather than 'only' his mother's words.*
> **Kate, Hero's Heart mom**

As an African proverb states, "it takes a village to raise a child." We need one another for support and our ancestors knew this. For thousands of years, a form of closeness existed within the human community that shaped our course as a species. We evolved by living in small, sustainable communities and sharing the central tasks of raising children. Indigenous people have held the wisdom of community, but for most of us reading this book, genuine community is sorely lacking and our need has become critical.

One of the greatest benefits of the Hero's Heart is the supportive community and loving relationships that are created among members. When you close your monthly circle with the benediction, the circle is open, but it is never broken. Members will maintain a loving connection throughout the month, developing a significant commitment to rejoice together, mourn together, and delight in each other. *The Hero's Heart* becomes a community that "does life together." In the chapter *Everything You Need to Know…*, I will show you how to build your own Hero's Heart community with other mothers who share similar concerns and values, and whose parenting style is to talk openly and directly about the passages our boys navigate on their journey to young manhood. On this journey, the impact of positive peer influences and an intentional community of other mothers and sons cannot be overstated. Hearing from other boys who are in a similar stage of life helps your son feel less alone and emboldens him to carry the insights he receives in circle with him into the world and put them into practice. Hearing from other mothers in circle offers our sons meaningful echoes of our own values through multiple channels, making it all the more likely to leave a lasting imprint on his heart. In the Hero's Heart community, our sons find strength and we find support.

The Gift of a Rite of Passage Ceremony

> *If we do not initiate our sons into manhood, they will burn the village down to feel the heat.*
> **African Proverb**

At its most fundamental level, a rite of passage is a ceremony or event that serves to mark the transition from one stage of life to another, connecting the individual to self, to others, and to the greater community. These important ceremonies support life changes and the sacred space between transitions, reminding us that we are part of something much larger than ourselves. Across time and place, cultures have conceived myriad practices and rituals to mark life transitions, especially the vulnerable transitions from childhood to adolescence, and adolescence to adulthood.

Unfortunately, in our modern industrial societies, meaningful rites of passage that clearly delineate the milestones on the journey to adulthood have all but disappeared. While some cultures and religious communities provide youth with meaningful initiatory rituals, Western secular culture has very little to offer the deep psychic needs of its young people. For the most part, our cultural milieu no longer offers young people a spiritual space that both acknowledges and informs their transition to adulthood. This loss may be more impactful than we realize.

According Dr. Richard Frankel, psychotherapist and author of *The Adolescent Psyche*, the process of initiation is an archetypal experience in our collective unconscious, and as such, it will manifest whether or not a given culture formally invests in rites of passage. What this means is that young people inherently crave customs that will mark, honor, and help them move through their coming of age years, so if the culture lacks meaningful initiatory rituals, children will subconsciously seek to fill the gaps themselves. Without the support of loving adults or the community in general, often what young people create for themselves as a rite of passage of sorts is fraught with chaos and danger. It has been theorized that the devastating epidemic among young people of alcohol and drug abuse, premature experimentation with sexual activity, teen pregnancies, and involvement in violence and gangs is at least partly the result of an unconscious desire for self-initiation. It is as if our children are saying, in multiple ways, "Please help me learn who I am, please lead the way, please show me my place in this great world." *The Hero's Heart* offers our sons the meaningful rite of passage they so deeply crave.

According to Gilbert H. Herdt, Professor of Human Sexuality Studies and Anthropology at San Francisco State University, and author of *Rituals of Manhood*, although rites of passage practices vary widely across cultures and continuously evolve, they all share the following universal themes and basic elements:

- Separation from society
- Preparation or instruction
- Transition (i.e. during adolescence, from child to adult)
- Welcoming back into society, acknowledging the change of status.

The Hero's Heart is a year-long, modern-day program designed to incorporate the four basic elements of a traditional coming-of-age rite of passage as described by Herdt.

The Hero's Heart:

- Utilizes the powerful vehicle of sacred circling, offering our sons space to **separate** from the restrictive limits of society while they find their own voices and define for themselves their own truths and meaning.
- Offers direct, holistic **instruction** that integrates psycho-emotional, social, and spiritual elements, sharing with our boys relevant and effective tools and perspectives that will help propel them toward a greater sense of personal wholeness as they navigate the teen years.
- Recognizes and honors the important life **transition** from childhood to adolescence.
- Culminates in a final ceremony designed to **welcome** the emergent young man into a community born of love, fellowship, and support, and to **acknowledge** his vital role in his family and community.

Growing up can feel scary and the years between boyhood and manhood are often fraught with confusion. Rites of passage give us strength, support, resources, space, and acknowledgment. When we consider the adolescent years and all the profound and often tumultuous experiences awaiting our sons just beyond the horizon, the Hero's Heart acts as potent preventative medicine. The final chapter of this book will walk you step-by-step through implementing your very own Hero's Heart rite of passage ceremony.

MOTHERS AND SONS, TOGETHER

❝ *I think togetherness is a very important ingredient to family life.*
Barbara Bush

So often we begin our mothering journey passionate about cultivating a secure attachment with our children, and then slowly along the way, the job gets harder, we lose our footing, and we start listening to the mainstream. Most mainstream writing and advising around parenting during the adolescent years focuses on the term "individuating," and instructs parents to pull back. There is a general fear and persistent myth that if we focus on remaining close with our children as they age, we will somehow hinder their growth as independent and self-sufficient beings. This pervasive cultural narrative does not reflect what science, and often our own intuition, tells us about what our teens really need to become healthy, independent adults. The truth is that what our children most need from us as their parents is for us to consistently hold them close because when a child's connection needs are fully met, they are ready to healthfully do the work of adolescence.

In his book, *Hold on to Your Kids: Why Parents Need to Matter More Than Peers*, author and developmental psychologist Gordon Neufeld describes the healthy process of individuation:

> *The key to activating maturation is to take care of the attachment needs of the child. To foster independence, we must first invite dependence; to promote individuation we must provide a sense of belonging and unity; to help the child separate we must assume responsibility for keeping the child close.*

Contrary to popular cultural mythology, it is not normal or healthy for our children to withdraw from us, and we as parents are wise to actively maintain and strengthen our connection with our growing children and teens. To be clear, this is not about "helicopter parenting" – when parents hover close and become over-involved in their child's every problem or decision. This is not about keeping them dependent on us, or dominating them. Nor is this about sheltering our adolescents, or about having our own needs met. This is about keeping our finger on the pulse of what is happening in their lives at the exact time that they are finding their own voices, planning their own futures, facing tremendous challenges, and striving to make sense of the world.

We possess some deep cultural wounds about what it means to "grow up", and these wounds pervade our relationships with our children. A trend exists in our culture of confusion about mothering as our children enter adolescence – especially regarding boys. Many parents, often with the best of intentions, have subconsciously abdicated their natural roles of guardians and guides of their children. Nowhere is this parental withdrawal more salient and common than in the relationship between mothers and sons.

Preserving the Relationship

A mother's connection to her son is commonly regarded as finite, an inevitable casualty of a boy's growth into manhood. The tacit message many of us have absorbed is that a well-adjusted, loving mother is one who gradually but surely pushes her son away, both emotionally and physically, in order to allow him to grow up to be a healthy man. Mothers get messages from very early on to push their boys away. The love of a mother – both the son's love for her and hers for him – is believed to "feminize" a boy, and in a culture that devalues the feminine, this equates to being seen as soft and weak. Of course, such gender stereotyping is lamentable because empathy, emotional aptitude, and the desire for intimate relationships are fundamentally human attributes. Importantly, there is no equivalent maxim for fathers and sons, or for mothers and daughters, to "cut the apron strings" (which literally means, "to stop support"). Thus, the patriarchal message is designed to strip women of one of the greatest powers we have – that of our ability to influence the status quo through our influence on the next generation of men.

Women participate in and perpetuate this lie as well. Even the most enlightened mother who cares about her son and wants the best for him can feel impelled by the cultural lie to "cut the apron strings," lest he turn out to be a "mama's boy", or worse, a "sissy." As Adrienne Rich has described, "the fear of alienating a male child from 'his' culture seems to go deep, even among women who reject that culture for themselves every day of their lives." In *Of Woman Born*, Rich challenges this thinking, "What do we fear? That our sons will accuse us of making them misfits and outsiders? That they will suffer as we have suffered from patriarchal reprisals? Do we fear that they will somehow lose their male status and privilege, even as we are seeking to abolish that inequality?"

Rather than causing harm, a boy's closeness with his mother actually works like preventative medicine. In a study of 426 boys through middle school, Carlos Santos, professor at Arizona State University's School of Social and Family Dynamics, found that boys who remain close to their mothers throughout the middle school years tend not to embrace hyper-masculine stereotypes, such as emotional stoicism and physical toughness, and instead are more emotionally intelligent. Closeness to fathers did not have the same effect. Using a mental health measure called the Children's Depression Inventory, Santos also observed that boys who shunned masculine stereotypes and remained more emotionally available had, on average, improved mental health throughout middle school.

I fundamentally believe a boy never loses his need to be understood and loved by his mother, and that there is no point – not at age five, or ten, or fifteen – when a boy must "give up" his mother, or when a mother must "give up" her son. What interests me is the creation of a new narrative, in which boys stay close to their mothers.

A Mother-Son Circle? YES! How Mothers Can (and Should) Lead Their Sons into Young Manhood

> *Despite the barrage of criticism and the constant admonitions to push their sons away, mothers have been engaging in their own underground social rebellion. They have been working hard to nurture the emotional skills they know their sons need.*
> **Kate Stone Lombardi, *The Mama's Boy Myth***

I trust that like me, you too wish to resist the cultural dictum and preserve the closeness you enjoy with your son. Perhaps you are seeking to repair or re-establish a hurting bond. Please know that I have created a powerful way for us to do this, but the first thing we must fully embrace is that – yes – our sons need their mothers to continue the journey with them, just as we always have, especially as they approach young manhood. We are the perfect ones for this sacred task! The bond a boy has with his mother is likely the most deeply rooted emotional connection in his early life. Most sons feel emotionally safest with their mothers and most mothers know their sons better than anyone else. The pieces of their hearts that our boys allow us to see are tender and precious, and we can handle and mold the hero's heart with confidence. And if by spending time in circle with us, our sons further develop some of the personality characteristics and values our culture classifies as feminine – for example, compassion, emotional expression, verbal communication, and nonviolence – then hurray! Because those are precisely the qualities our sons need to grow into healthy, whole adults with satisfying relationships.

What About the Fathers?

There is no doubt that our sons need their fathers just as much as they need their mothers. Let me be clear: *The Hero's Heart* is not meant to be a replacement for father-son experiences, programs, or general bonding. In fact, most of the boys who have participated in my Hero's Heart circle offerings, including my own beloved sons, have had tremendously active and involved fathers. What *The Hero's Heart* does is empower mothers to also actively guide their adolescent sons into young manhood.

Recent generations have seen that fathers who live with their children are taking an increasingly active role in caring for them, and the ranks of "stay-at-home" and single fathers have grown significantly in recent decades. Separately, more children around the world are growing up without an involved father. What about those boys? They are left with a void, and their mothers are burdened with worry and guilt for what their sons do not have. I believe single mothers, rather than wasting energy wringing their hands and trying to orchestrate a passing relationship with a male athletic coach or teacher, would most benefit their sons by directing their energy toward themselves and assume the primary role of leading their sons into young manhood. That is what this book is saying: *mothers, you do not have to wait for fathers, or cajole men in the community, to lead your sons. Just as a loving, conscious father can surely guide his daughter into empowered and healthy young womanhood, you too are equipped for the task.*

The luckiest of sons have a wealth of elders, both men and women, mothers and fathers. The challenges faced by boys today are considerable, and boys benefit from having a plurality of adults in positions of advocacy and mentorship. As the creator and author of *The Hero's Heart*, I give my wholehearted, emphatic blessing to any father (or mixed mother/father group) who wishes to modify or adapt the curriculum for their use.

Perhaps one day, our sons, so impacted by the experience of sharing sacred circle with their mothers as adolescents, will grow into men that continue to seek or create the practice of sacred circling in their own lives and with their own sons (and daughters.) And perhaps, when that day comes, they will return to this book.

WIDENING THE CIRCLE: SHARING THE PRACTICE OF SACRED CIRCLING WITH OUR SONS

The circle is a return to our original form of community as well as a leap forward to create a new form of community.
Christina Baldwin, *Calling the Circle*

A circle is a sacred symbol that has been honored throughout time to represent limitless possibilities – love with no beginning and no end. Throughout the ages, people from all walks of life, religions, political systems, and cultures have gathered in sacred circles to co-create community and to collaborate in the forming of a shared life experience. Circling may feel novel to us, but this is an ancient practice with roots going back tens of thousands of years.

What is Sacred Circling?

As Christina Baldwin explains in *Calling the Circle*, "A circle is not just a meeting with the chairs rearranged. A circle is a way of doing things differently than we have become accustomed to." The magic of the Hero's Heart lies in this unique approach. I will explore this "way of doing things" below.

The Key Ingredients of a Sacred Circle:

1. **Sanctity.** Circle time is meant to be protected. As we enter circle, we step away from our daily routine and enter a place of healing, blessing, and replenishing. We bind an agreement, both spoken and unspoken, to hold each other and the gathering itself as

sacred. When we enter circle, we come with love, consciousness, honor, and respect. We set our intention for a soulful, bonding, and heart-opening experience. Although the term *sacred* is used to describe this practice, there is no particular religious or spiritual path or belief system implied. Sacred circling is for Christians, Jews, atheists, Buddhists, Muslims, Hindus, people of any religious persuasion and those with none whatsoever. In practice, the atmosphere of love and peace is so palpable that almost every circle member recognizes a spiritual experience (even agnostic or atheist members), and sons naturally recognize and appreciate these reverent aspects.

2. **Safety.** Trust is paramount. As Maslow's hierarchy of needs theory explains, for deep sharing, learning, close relationships, and personal growth to germinate, one must first and fundamentally feel safe. Circle offers an explicitly secure environment where we are supported and emotionally safe. In circle, we trust that our personal stories will be protected with the strictest confidence. We do not share the words, information, or stories of another circle member with anyone outside the circle.

3. **Witnessing.** Listening is loving. In circle, we act as sacred witnesses for one another's process. What this means is that we simply hold space for what *is*. In concrete terms, this means that when a mother or son shares a check-in or responds to a discussion question, we listen with our full heart and mind; we offer our full attention. When the speaker finishes, we do not respond with cross-talk, advice, fixing, "what I would do is," or referrals. With acceptance and honor we simply say, "Thank you for sharing your heart/wisdom/experience/story/thoughts/feelings with us." By offering gratitude for the speaker's process, we trust that we naturally bend toward healing like a flower to the sunlight. We do not have to do some deed to effect positive change in another's life. The simple and sacred act of observation can guide our circle partners to new truths.

4. **Authenticity.** To feel bonded, we must feel seen. On the stone pathway to the gathering place of the original Hero's Heart circle rests a sign that reads: "Just show up." Authenticity is letting what we are experiencing on the inside "show up" on the outside. Authenticity is courageously uncovering and expressing how we deeply feel. Our deeper, tender feelings are a large part of what makes us human, and circle holds space for this authentic sharing. In circle, we practice pausing, going within, taking a breath and acknowledging how we truly feel before we speak, so that we may find the earnest expressions that connect us in more fulfilling ways to ourselves and to others. Circle says, "come, show up and be exactly who you are, exactly where you are in your life, at this moment." Feeling the unconditional love and acceptance of circle, members feel safe enough to remove any social masks and allow their authentic selves be seen. In circle, we are completely free to be ourselves.

5. **Inclusivity.** Circle is inclusive of all forms of diversity. All are welcome and individual differences are celebrated. There is room in circle for many opinions, voices, and views. We are committed to not letting our differences divide us or blind us to our ultimate commonalities. We trust that everyone has something of value to offer the whole. Circle has a true power like that of alchemy that transforms our differences into a golden synergy where, as Aristotle wrote, "The whole is greater than the sum of its parts."

6. **Silence.** Silence is meaningful. Consider how in a musical composition, the pauses or moments of rest imbue the music with beauty and shape. Without silence there is no music; there is only noise. By recognizing the silences within our circle discussion and embracing those soft moments, we connect more deeply to ourselves and to one another. In circle, silence is valued for allowing us to ruminate on what was said and discover what will be given voice to next as it emerges in the present moment. Silence offers an opportunity to unearth the mysteries and lessons that exist within and allows for individuals to integrate their experience, staying grounded and engaged. When a circle member honors the voice of silence and the power to not speak by choosing to pass the talking stick, we offer thanks in the same manner as when one shares from the heart with words. Welcoming silence requires practice because many of us instinctively feel uneasy when encountering pauses or interruptions in flow and we often feel a compulsion to fill a perceived void. In circle, we know this is not necessary and we resist the habit of filling silent periods with superficial talk. Silence, as the old saying goes, is golden.

7. **Ritual.** Circle reclaims ritual. For many people today, the word 'ritual' is a loaded term and conjures up images of exotic religions or the occult. Others may believe that rituals are something only ordained priests or ministers can access and create. In actuality, *anyone* – from any religious path or belief system or none – can participate in and benefit from circle ritual. Circle rituals are essentially design elements that focus the group on their interconnection with one another and on something greater than themselves. At the Hero's Heart, a simple candlelight ritual is shared at the closing of each circle to carry this reminder.

8. **Co-creation.** Just as we co-create our experience of life, we co-create our experience of circle. There is no hierarchy in circle and all participants, including one or two facilitators have a precisely equal role in the process. Each circle co-creates its own powerful synergy, which would not be possible without each member's specific participation and unique offerings. As we say in *The Hero's Heart* agreements (explained in Part II), "We are all the teachers, and we are all the taught."

Widening the Circle

The 1990s saw a strong resurgence of sacred circling among women, who longed for an emotionally safe haven where values considered feminine were not only tolerated, but celebrated. Women's sacred circles have since become a prominent force of individual and social change. Women are gathering in circles of support for each other in healing circles, wisdom circles, soul sister circles. Circles of mothers and daughters together, of community mothers, of grandmothers. My first circle creation and offering, *The Heroines Club*, was born from this wave of inspiration of female empowerment.

However, the practice of sacred circling itself is not gender specific and need not be considered exclusive to women and girls. Indeed, one of the most successful "sacred circles" in America and probably the world, Alcoholics Anonymous, is comprised of both women and men. After nearly thirty years from the beginning of the women's spirituality movement, mothers are ready and the time is right to widen the circle and extend this gift to our sons.

The ultimate goal and core intention of the Hero's Heart is to create a loving community invested in guiding and supporting our sons. The practice of sacred circling offers us a direct and proven path to achieving this noble mission. Sacred circles afford an atmosphere of discovery and growth not found elsewhere in contemporary culture: an environment free of hierarchy and competition, which serves as the perfect conduit for the learning, empowerment, healing, communication, community building, and interconnection that our sons so desperately need right now.

Groups of mothers and sons join together in genuine community through the deliberate design of a sacred circle. The functioning of a group as a sacred circle and the achievement of true community does require energy and attention and following some general principles. In Part II, I will explain how this evolves in practice and walk you through how to best promote the fundamental precepts of a healthy sacred circle to your own Hero's Heart mother-son circle.

PART II

EVERYTHING YOU NEED TO KNOW TO SET UP YOUR CIRCLE AND KEEP IT STRONG

Setting Up Your Circle

The previous chapters have laid the foundation on which to build your circle. Now we will consider the framework and structures needed to keep your circle strong and enduring. Whether you are planning an intimate gathering of just a couple of other mothers and sons or are envisioning to bring the gift of *The Hero's Heart* to your larger community, building and sustaining a successful Hero's Heart circle requires some conscious planning. Here are the most important questions you will want to consider before your first circle ever meets.

Who will lead?

In the methodology of *The Hero's Heart*, there are one or two dedicated facilitators planning and guiding the circle. The role of the facilitator is to develop a safe and empowering environment that brings about sincere contributions from the participants. Having one or two mothers fill this role consistently typically yields good results. However, if a group of mothers wants to share the responsibility, these duties can be rotated among members, or shared in some other way, as long as everyone is committed. Being an effective facilitator is a learned skill and an intuitive art, and a role for which any woman is qualified, should she feel called.

The responsibilities of the facilitator are to: plan and prepare for the circle (using the curriculum as a guide), create an environment where participants can flourish, and guide discussions to maintain focus and depth, while honoring both the flow of the group and the time boundaries.

Who will be invited?

Time and again, it has been my experience that the people who are meant for this kind of experience are the ones drawn to it, and each mother and son who chooses to participate is there for a reason. With this in mind, choosing whom to invite is an important consideration as the health and longevity of your circle is largely determined by the cohesion of the circle as a whole. Diversity of race, religion, socioeconomic status, and so forth is desirable, as people with different backgrounds, skills, attitudes and experiences will bring fresh ideas and perceptions. What is essential is that despite those differences, all of the mothers are united in their vision for the circle. Of utmost importance is that the mothers share similar values and are in accordance about the purpose of the Hero's Heart circle.

When all mothers have the same foundation it becomes easier to discuss issues – both logistical and philosophical – and to know what the Hero's Heart journey will entail. For this reason, each mother should read at least Part I of this book before committing to joining the circle. Having this as a prerequisite for participation will ensure a good fit between mothers, while providing a strong base of shared knowledge and inspiration for those women who will be joining your circle.

What will be the age range of sons?

The Hero's Heart curriculum is designed with boys aged 9–14 in mind. However, for a given circle it is recommended to have somewhat narrow age range of less than a few years as the needs of the sons and the nature of the discussions evolve as boys grow and mature. At the same time, having some age variation optimizes the educative potential for all, as the younger boys learn from the older boys, and the older boys have an opportunity to strengthen their leadership skills.

An age range of 9–11 or 12–14 years old is usually just right. Of course, many other factors are just as important as chronological age when considering who will participate (maturity level, desire to participate, friendships, sibling dynamics), and I encourage you to trust your intuition here.

What is an ideal circle size?

Since the Hero's Heart explores personal issues and matters of the heart, a small, more intimate circle is best. From experience, I have found that a circle of five to seven pairs (ten to fourteen people) is just right. This number of participants is enough to stimulate discussion, but not so many as to intimidate quieter members, or compromise privacy or emotional safety.

What will be the investment from the participants?

The Hero's Heart is not a 'for-profit' venture; instead we aim that each member feels her investment is met with equal return, so that all may benefit together.

The investments required to implement a successful Hero's Heart circle include:

TIME AND ENERGY

- To plan for each monthly circle using the curriculum as your guide.

- To buy, gather, create, and prepare the needed supplies for each monthly circle.

- To prepare the space before, and to clean the space after, each monthly circle.

- To implement the curriculum and facilitate the circle through an empowering, bonding, and heart-opening experience.

MONEY

- To purchase Integrated Activity supplies.

- To purchase snacks and refreshments (as desired).

- To purchase ritual candles, Journey Journals, and talking stick (as desired).

The total investment of time, energy, and financial costs associated with the Hero's Heart should be factored into the overall exchange among members and explicitly agreed upon at the outset. There are many creative ways to address the investment among participants. For the health and longevity of your circle, it is absolutely necessary to give this careful thought and to be clear on this from the beginning.

The financial cost associated with providing the supplies needed for the monthly Integrated Activities ranges from $300-$500 total for the year, depending on what supplies you already have on hand and the number of participants in your circle. An equitable approach is to divide that amount among the number of participants, and require each member to contribute a "supply fee" prior to beginning the circle, which the facilitator will use solely for the purchasing of supplies.

In addition to the financial investment for supplies, the amount of time, energy, and attention the facilitator offers the circle must be compensated in some way, so as not to create a situation that breeds exhaustion, burnout, or resentment. I cannot emphasize the importance of this enough. For many of us, this will be challenging because it can feel incredibly uncomfortable to ask for money to do the things we are good at doing, want to do, or enjoy doing – especially if it involves close friends. For the health of your circle, the facilitator should create healthy boundaries and expectations to ensure that she is not doing it all with little return. The facilitator needs to receive energy, in order to give of her energy fully without experiencing burnout. This can be accomplished by dividing facilitator tasks and responsibilities among mothers, charging an additional fee to compensate the facilitator for her time and energy, or bartering with the facilitator in some fashion.

There is no absolutely right or wrong way to address the investment among participants. The early iterations of the Hero's Heart agreed to a $25 cost per circle, amounting to $300 per year for each mother-son pair. This covered all supply fees as well as compensated for the time, energy, and attention of the facilitator. In return for this financial investment, mothers and sons had no additional responsibilities other than to show up and receive.

Each circle will be unique, and what feels right for one, may not for another. I encourage you to practice sovereignty in deciding what feels good and fair for you and your circle. Finally, a truth I have learned is this: others will only value our time and energy if we demonstrate that we value our time and energy.

Where will your circle gather?

The setting for your circle sets the tone for the experience. The meeting space should feel dedicated, cozy, and safe. I recommend meeting in a private office space or in quiet areas of members' homes. Above all, the space you choose should feel physically comfortable and allow for close connection, while protecting the circle from any outside intrusion or unnecessary distractions. If you are renting a space for the circles, this charge and the administration involved (collecting keys, etc.) needs to be factored into the payment and responsibilities.

What will be the frequency and duration of circle gatherings?

The Hero's Heart curriculum is designed to be a once-a-month gathering, spanning the course of one year. However, some circles may choose to take off the summer or holiday months to allow for travel and other plans. Different circles will have different preferences and the curriculum can be adapted to meet various schedule needs and desires.

The duration of the circle, given all of its elements, can last anywhere from one and a half to two hours. Crucial to the health of the circle is to consistently honor the planned time boundaries. This means that circle members trust that circle will start on time and end on time. To ensure this happens, I recommend creating an explicit agreement between the mothers in advance that each circle will begin and end at precisely designated times. If a member arrives late to circle, they are invited to quietly enter and take their seats in the circle in progress. Periodically throughout the circle, the facilitator will confirm that the rhythm and pace is on track, making adjustments as needed, to honor the agreed upon end time.

Keeping Your Circle Healthy and Strong

There are some common growing pains that your circle may encounter, and by anticipating and communicating about them, your circle will remain healthy, strong, and sustainable. I recommend the following measures to prevent circle deterioration and to maintain overall enthusiasm and goodwill.

Review the agreements at every circle

The Hero's Heart agreements will be explained in detail in the next chapter. It is helpful to open every circle with a reading of the rules to serve as a reminder of the agreed upon commitments.

Periodic "health of the circle" check-ins

Seasonally, either in person or online, hold space for any sharing and reflection regarding the health of the circle as a whole.

- How are the commitments being honored?
- How is the circle as a whole serving the members?
- Is there anything that needs to be addressed?
- Is there anything not working anymore?

Even if things are running smoothly, this preventative measure will promote group cohesion and ensure continued vitality.

Maintain connection between circles

Some of the greatest benefits of the Hero's Heart are the supportive community and loving relationships created among members. When you close your monthly circle with the benediction, the circle is open, but it is never broken: members will maintain a loving connection with one another throughout the month. This connection can be supported by continuing contact with one another through social gatherings, online, and by attending special events. The Hero's Heart circles I facilitate make a special point of inviting one another to their athletic games, theatrical performances, birthday parties, etc. There are many creative ways that your circle can maintain connection and continue to grow closer between circle gatherings. It is a worthwhile endeavor to cultivate this connection in ways that feel supportive to all.

When someone leaves the circle

Despite the best intentions from the beginning, lives and circumstances change and sometimes even the most committed circle will lose a mother-son pair along the way.

The Hero's Heart circle is co-created among all members: each mother-son pair brings something special to the circle that would not exist without their presence. Like a hanging mobile, when one part changes or moves, the other pieces also shift position. When this happens, it is helpful to honor the change with a simple ritual to acknowledge the circle's evolution and to lovingly release the departing mother and son from the circle.

The bonds formed between circle members strengthen over the course of the year, and the understanding of how the circle "works" is learned together as the year progresses. Therefore, depending on when a membership change occurs, it may or may not feel appropriate to replace members. As with everything, let your heart and intuition be your guide and discuss it openly together.

Dealing with conflict between members

The Hero's Heart is a very intimate experience, and there are no substantive human relationships that are completely free from conflict. In fact, conflict can be healthy as every person in our lives acts as a mirror for us, reflecting parts of ourselves back to us, and offering an opportunity to grow. In her book, *Calling the Circle,* Christina Baldwin recommends considering the following questions if you find yourself feeling provoked or thinking negatively about another circle member:

- *How have I been pulled off center?*
- *What's my body telling me?*
- *What's my mind telling my body?*
- *Whose shadow work is this? And how do I own my piece with integrity?*
- *Who does this person remind me of?*
- *Am I seeing this situation through a filter of a past memory? Of judgment? Of fear?*

After considering these questions, if the matter remains an issue, open and honest communication among members may be needed. In my experience, the Hero's Heart has had very little serious conflict, perhaps from luck or perhaps due to the personalities of the members that are drawn to this kind of experience. Regardless, if your circle encounters conflict, it is best to use an authentic, heart-centered approach, allowing each member to share their thoughts and feelings, while owning their experience and speaking from the first-person "I" perspective.

IMPLEMENTING
THE HERO'S HEART CURRICULUM

Part III of this book offers twelve complete circle templates, in addition to the Mothers' Circle and the Rite of Passage Ceremony, to guide you through one full year of facilitating your very own Hero's Heart circle. Here, we will explore in detail how to implement the monthly templates to offer the mothers and sons of your community a positive, heart-opening and empowering experience.

Are you ready to make your own Hero's Heart magic? The first thing to consider is how to prepare the setting to establish the tone for your sacred mother-son circle.

Preparing the Environment

The space that the mothers and sons first enter sets the tone for the circle and speaks to the expectations of circle behavior without saying a word. Mothers and sons instinctively know they are stepping into a place of reverence, safety, and self-exploration by the way the room is arranged, organized, and decorated. Consider the following elements when preparing the space for your Hero's Heart gathering:

1. SEATING

Sitting in a sacred mother-son circle entails – you guessed it – sitting in a circle! The circular seating arrangement reflects the egalitarian nature of the Hero's Heart, while encouraging discussion and familiarity. Seating should be physically comfortable and promote mother-son bonding. Couches are great for this, as well as floor cushions and abundant pillows. Mothers and sons should be invited and encouraged to sit beside one another.

2. LIGHTING

Lighting sets the mood. Our bodies respond energetically to the color and intensity of the light around us, and our emotions respond accordingly. Most upscale, romantic restaurants keep the lighting low and provide candlelight for a reason: soft, warm lighting encourages relaxation and intimacy, and aids in the release of oxytocin, a key hormone for bonding. Consider turning off any bright overhead lights, and gently illuminate the space with lamps and candlelight.

3. ALTAR

Altars have been used for thousands of years as places to express creativity, access intuition, reflect on thoughts and ideas of personal importance and value, and connect with the divine of your understanding. We all create altars, whether we recognize it or not. For example, most of us have special places in our homes where we lovingly set family photos, mementos, and natural items we cherish. Your Hero's Heart altar is a physical representation of your intentions for the circle and it serves as a beautifully designed focus for the eyes to gaze throughout circle. Place a coffee table or other small table to serve as an altar in the center of your circle. If you are all sitting on the floor, you may wish to use a special quilt or cloth for this purpose so as to have the altar at everyone's eye level. On the altar, place the talking stick and a large candle. Invite the circle to bring items to place on the altar that represent the month's Affirmation: photographs, items from nature, gemstones, small family heirlooms, books, drawings etc.

4. MUSIC

Music affects mood. Instrumental background music played quietly as mothers and sons enter the space encourages relaxation and tranquility.

5. SCENTS

Our sense of smell has a tremendous impact on our feelings and behaviors. For example, can you remember an experience of entering someone's home and meeting the pleasant smell of freshly-baked cookies? Chances are, the aroma elicited feelings of coziness, leading you to want to relax and befriend.

In circle, we can use the power of fragrance as a tool to help participants transition from everyday life into the sacredness of circle. Because smell is so closely linked with memory, through repeated exposure to the same scent, members begin to associate the aroma with positive behaviors and feelings of safety and love. Consider burning the same dried herb, wood, or incense (white sage, sweetgrass, cedar, lavender, palo santo, etc.) in the gathering space as participants arrive. As soon as members walk into the room and smell the "signature scent" of your circle, the emotional tone will be set.

6. REFRESHMENTS

From my experience, the boys are always really excited about the snacks! Consider providing drinks and a special snack. This could be an area where the responsibility is shared among members, with a different mother-son pair providing snacks for the circle each month. Or, you may decide to skip this part all together! That's fine too. Try not to disrupt the earnestness of the talking circle, and consider serving snacks during the transition to the Integrated Activity.

7. TALKING STICK

The Talking Stick was a tool used by Native Americans to let everyone speak their mind during a council meeting. According to the Native American tradition, the stick was imbued with spiritual qualities that called up the spirit of their ancestors to guide them in making good decisions. The stick ensured that all members who wished to speak had their ideas heard and that all members of the circle were valued equally.

With gratitude and honor for this Native American tradition, consider incorporating a talking stick into your circle to keep the discussion balanced among all participants. During check-ins and discussion, the talking stick is passed around the circle from member to member, allowing only the person holding the stick to speak. Whoever holds the talking stick has within their hands the sacred power of words, and the other circle members direct their full attention to the speaker, remaining silent and practicing sacred witnessing. This enables all those present in circle to have an opportunity to be heard, regardless of personality style or feelings of shyness. Of course, circle members are also welcomed to choose to pass the stick and *not* speak, as silence has a powerful energy as well.

You may wish to fashion your own talking stick or use some other item, such as a feather, to serve as a symbolic talking stick for your circle. Whatever the object, it carries respect for truth-telling and assures the speaker they have the freedom and power to say what is in their heart.

Letters to the Mothers

Each month's template begins with a letter written directly to the Hero's Heart mothers that offers an introduction to the theme for the month and an exploration of why the topic is so important for our sons. This is meant to be read prior to the monthly gathering to help mothers prepare their own hearts and minds for the topic discussion.

Affirmations

Each month's topic is encapsulated by a positive Affirmation. The monthly Affirmations provided are designed to inspire, energize, and motivate. Through these statements, we affirm that the value, idea, action, or skill we are discussing that month is both true and present in our hearts, thus supporting that reality.

Journey Journals

Every important journey deserves to be recorded, and the Hero's Heart year is no different! At the start of the circle year, provide each member with a new, personal journal to capture their experiences. At the beginning of each circle, invite participants to turn to a fresh page, and write the date and current Affirmation at the top. Any questions, feelings, thoughts, ideas, special moments, or important information from circle can be recorded in the Journey Journals. Additionally, some of the monthly Integrated Activities require writing in the Journey Journals, and members will record their chosen quote from the Quote Study in their Journey Journal each month. At the end of each circle gathering, the facilitator will remind the group of the Heartwork assignments for that month, and participants may wish to write them down in their journal as a reminder. For these reasons, members are expected to bring their journals with them to each circle and keep them on their home altar in between circles. At the end of the Hero's Heart Coming of Age year, mothers and sons will have a treasured memento of the extraordinary journey that was shared.

Each Month's Circle Journey: The Sequence of Events

The sequence of events for each Hero's Heart circle should remain consistent throughout the year. Just as when our sons were little and benefited from being read the same picture books over and over, when we provide a routine and predictable circle structure, sons will feel safe and secure enough to dive deep within themselves and the circle experience. The following table covers the recommended sequence of events, time allotments, purpose of each event, and suggestions for successful implementation every step of the way.

EVENT	TIME
Welcoming	Starting 15 minutes before circle begins
Opening Meditation	3 minutes
Reading of the Agreements	1 minute
Check-ins	15 to 20 minutes
Introduction of Affirmation and Topic	5 minutes
Discussion Prompts	30 minutes
Integrated Activities and Check-ins	30 minutes
Quote Study	10 minutes
Heartwork and Announcements	5 minutes
Candlelight Ritual and Song	5 minutes
Closing Benediction	1 minute

Welcoming

Mothers and sons should be greeted warmly and with enthusiasm, welcoming them into circle and inviting them to make themselves comfortable.

This time can also be used to briefly touch base and to share any important information with mothers and sons as they arrive. The facilitator may wish to provide suggestions for what to do before circle begins (find a seat together, place any items you may have brought on the altar, make yourselves comfortable, help yourselves to refreshments, etc.)

Opening Meditation

The opening meditation officially commences the circle. The purpose is to invite mothers and sons to relax into the space, begin to synchronize with one another energetically, set their intentions for what they hope to emotionally give and receive during circle, and bring their body, mind, and heart fully into the present moment.

The following meditation can be used verbatim, or feel free to use this as a guide and create your own.

I invite you to find a comfortable, fully-supported resting position and gently close your eyes. You may wish to cuddle up with your mother or with your son, or you may wish to hold hands with one another. Begin to notice your breath. Not trying to change anything, just observe the natural rhythm of your breath. Now, breathe deeply and feel the oxygen as it travels into your body, relaxing you even more as it fills you with new life. Allow any tension in your body to gently melt away with each deep, cleansing breath.

I invite you to 'press pause' on all of the activities and responsibilities occurring outside of this time and space, and land fully present in this moment, this sweet, special time you have carved out and reserved to spend with your beloved son, with your mother. What do you hope to receive from our time here together? What do you hope to give? In this next gentle pause, silently set your intentions for our time together. Thank you for being here with us. Your presence in circle is a gift to us all and we are grateful to be sharing the Hero's Heart journey with you. Enjoy a few more gentle, cleansing breaths, and when you are ready, open your eyes.

A Reading of the Agreements

PURPOSE

Each circle begins with a reading of the commitments to remind the circle of the agreed upon expectations, as well as to allow each participant an opportunity to use their voice and become comfortable speaking in circle.

SUGGESTIONS

A written copy of the Hero's Heart agreements should be passed around the circle, with each participant reading a tenet. Continue passing the copy around until all the commitments have been read. The Hero's Heart agreements are:

- *We are all the teachers and we are all the taught.*
- *We share from our hearts and speak our truths.*
- *What is said in circle stays in circle.*
- *We respect the space.*
- *We honor ourselves, one another, and the mother-son relationship.*

Check-ins

Check-ins provide an opportunity for mothers and sons to experience a sense of belonging to the group and reestablish the connection among members.

Pass the talking stick around the circle, inviting each participant to share how they are feeling and their response to a check-in prompt. This is also the time to share any stories, insights, or reactions from the previous month's Heartwork.

Use a different, engaging check-in prompt each month. Have fun and get creative with this! Potential check-in prompts could be:

- *Something you are particularly proud of about yourself this month.*
- *Something you are grateful for right now.*
- *Something you and your mother/son have in common.*
- *Something you really appreciate about your mother/ son.*
- *Something you are excited about right now.*
- *Something you really like about yourself.*
- *Something you like about the Hero's Heart.*

Affirmation and Topic Introduction

To generate inspiration for the topic and ensure every circle member has the same basic knowledge of the month's topic and Affirmation, open your discussion by reading the Topic Introduction.

The facilitator should read the Topic Introduction section of that month's curriculum for all to hear, with feeling and eye contact as appropriate.

Discussion Prompts

PURPOSE

The Discussion Prompts provided each month are designed to generate conversation about the month's topic and Affirmation, as well as to provide mothers and sons an opportunity to bond together and to get to know one another on an even deeper level.

SUGGESTIONS

There are more Discussion Prompts provided each month than your circle will likely need. Use the questions that most resonate with the developmental level and interests of your circle. Leave space for silence and follow the flow of your circle to know when to move on to the next question. The talking stick can be useful for this element of circle.

Integrated Activity

PURPOSE

The Integrated Activities provided each month allow for a fun, concrete application of that month's Affirmation.

SUGGESTIONS

Follow the directions provided for each month's Integrated Activity.

Quote Study

PURPOSE

The quotes provided each month were selected for their potency, applicability, universality and dialogue potential for mothers and sons. The purpose of the Quote Study is to consider how we might apply the wisdom to our own lives and understanding.

Write each of the provided quotes on a separate slip of paper, fold and place them in a small basket or bowl. Photocopies of the quotes can be made and used directly from this book.

Pass the basket or bowl around the circle, inviting each participant to choose a quote. Mothers and sons will then pair up with one another and share their quotes, write them in their Journey Journals, and discuss the meaning and any life applications that can be made. After a few minutes (or when the conversations begin to wane), call the circle back together and allow time for each participant to share their quote and any insights that were gleaned from their private mother-son discussions.

Heartwork and Announcements/Requests

PURPOSE

Each month's curriculum includes recommendations for Heartwork (homework for the heart) for both sons and mothers to help build a bridge between what was shared, learned, and discovered in circle and everyday life.

To support the relationships and sense of community among members, hold space for announcements (important personal events, birthdays, sports games, theatrical events, social gatherings, etc.) and requests (prayer/positive vibes/send love requests, requests for specific help or support, etc.)

SUGGESTIONS

Read the Heartwork suggestions from the chapter and encourage circle members to write the assignments in their Journey Journals as a reminder.

Hold space for any brief announcements or appropriate requests.

Candlelight Ritual and Song

PURPOSE

The candlelight ritual and song symbolize our interconnection with one another and remind the circle that everyone has an inner light – a connection to the divine of your understanding and a higher purpose for your life – and it is our responsibility to follow that light by doing our best, being true to ourselves, and helping other people.

Provide a small taper candle for each circle participant. These can be actual candles, or if safety is a concern, battery-operated LED taper candles work well too. If you are using real candles, provide drip protectors, which can be found at most craft stores.

As a circle, sing the song *The Light Within*, by John Kramer (2010). You may wish to provide written lyrics for the first few gatherings until the circle is familiar with the song. An audio recording of the song can be obtained online at **https://MeliaKeetonDigby.com**

> *May the light within you shine before you,*
>
> *Every day, every day,*
>
> *May the light within you shine before you,*
>
> *Guide your way, guide your way,*
>
> *May the love we share surround you,*
>
> *And chase your fears away,*
>
> *May the light within you shine before you.*

As the circle sings together, mothers and sons will approach the altar in pairs, lighting their candles from the large altar candle that has been burning throughout the circle. Continue singing the song until every mother/son pair has lit their candles.

Closing

PURPOSE

The circle is closed with a benediction to seal in the experience that was shared together and to affirm the gifts received at the Hero's Heart.

SUGGESTIONS

With the ritual candles still lit, recite *The Hero's Heart* benediction together. At the end of the benediction, everyone will blow out their candles and the sacred circle for that month will be closed. You may wish to provide a written copy of the benediction to circle members for the first few gatherings, or until the benediction is memorized.

The Hero's Heart Benediction

May we love ourselves.

May we love each other.

May we believe that our dreams can come true.

May we work to make the world a better place.

We are strong.

We are wise.

We are the heroes of our own lives.

PART III

MOTHERS' ORGANIZATIONAL AND INTENTION-SETTING CIRCLE:
"I AM A CO-CREATOR"

> *Never doubt that a small group of thoughtful, committed citizens can change the world;*
> *indeed, it's the only thing that ever has.*
> **Margaret Mead**

Dear Mothers,

Congratulations and well done! You heard the call and took the leap to create your own Hero's Heart circle for your sons. You gathered the women, found the space, determined the schedule, and made the commitment. You have done the groundwork. And now, arm in arm, you are poised to take the first step on this blessed Hero's Heart journey together.

Prior to your first Hero's Heart circle with your sons, the organizational and intention-setting circle allows time for you as mothers to meet with one another and discuss expectations for circle participation, set and share intentions for what each mother hopes to gain from this experience with her son, and also have the opportunity to share anything they would like the circle to know about them or about their sons. This initial mothers-only circle is extremely powerful and special as it generates excitement for the upcoming year, and establishes a bond between the mothers that will continue to strengthen with each circle.

Offering somewhat of a dress rehearsal, this mothers-only circle should follow the typical sequence of events of the mother-son circles (delineated and described in the chapter *Implementing The Hero's Heart Curriculum*). After sharing a warm welcome, begin with a simple opening meditation, followed by a reading of the agreements, and a general check-in utilizing the talking stick (perhaps in response to the question, "Why did you feel inspired to join this circle?"). Next, introduce the Affirmation and topic, explore the discussion prompts, and share the integrated activity and quote study. Finally, just as you will in circle each month with your boys, close the circle with the candle ritual and song, followed by The Hero's Heart Benediction. Having moved through the format and flow of circle once together in advance, mothers will be better prepared to next usher their sons into and through the experience.

This mothers' circle is designed to address both the "nuts and bolts" of planning, as well as the "heart and soul" of intention-setting. It becomes easier to discuss issues – both logistical and philosophical – when all mothers have the same information as their foundation. For this reason, it is recommended that each mother reads Part I and Part II of this book in advance. Together, participants will co-create an evening of meaningful thought, necessary discussion, and inspired connections.

Every blessing on your journey.

We are in this together.

Love, *Melia*

Topic Introduction

Beloved mothers, welcome to the Hero's Heart! We are a circle of women who gather together for the divine work of blessing and guiding our sons, and in doing so, we join a worldwide grassroots movement to create the society in which we most wish to live. Our Affirmation for this mothers' circle is "*I Am a Co-Creator.*" What this means is that each of us has a precisely equal role and responsibility here and only by creating *together* will we manifest our highest hopes and dreams for this circle.

Did you ever play the parachute game at school when you were younger? Do you remember the special feeling when you and your classmates, each holding your own equally-spaced handle, lifted the parachute high above your heads, stepped forward, and then sat down on your edge of the parachute, creating a magical cathedral or circus tent above you? If one person accidentally dropped her handle during the maneuver, however, the tent would fall flat and not reach its fullness. In the same way, the magic we are co-creating for our sons requires that we each invest in the process. This mothers' circle is designed to help us establish what this means for us as a circle. We will take this time to talk through circle details and expectations, share our dreams and intentions, and bless this upcoming mother-son experience.

Raising our children is one of the great honors and responsibilities we have in life. We are guiding the men of tomorrow and it is such a blessing to be doing it together. Thank you for entering into my life and for allowing me the privilege of entering into yours. The ripples of what we are co-creating here together will extend far beyond what we can even imagine.

Discussion Prompts

1. In the chapter *What Our Sons Need Most*, the gifts of the Hero's Heart circle experience are listed as: quality time, sacred space to reconnect with ourselves, authenticity, close interpersonal relationships, communication skills, emotional intelligence, a healthy self-concept, values, information, purpose and meaning, community, and a rite of passage ceremony. Which of these gifts do you think will mean the most to your son and why? Which means the most to you?

2. Your circle's strength and effectiveness depend upon upholding the precepts of sacred circling. Earlier, in *Widening the Circle,* these precepts are listed as: sanctity, safety, witnessing, authenticity, inclusivity, silence, ritual, and co-creation. Which of these concepts feel particularly inspiring or meaningful to you? Which feel challenging? Both as an individual and as a circle whole, how might you ensure that these bedrock principles are honored?

3. For the overall health and longevity of your circle, what expectations for behavior and participation are important to communicate and agree upon? For example, arriving to circle on time, circle beginning and ending at the agreed upon times, mothers reading each month's chapter beforehand, minimizing and communicating any absences, mediating conflict among members, etc.

4. Considering the investments required to implement a successful Hero's Heart circle (planning, buying/gathering/creating/preparing supplies, preparing the space before circle and cleaning it after, facilitating the circle, snacks, etc.) how will your circle address the investment among members? How will the total investment of time, energy, and financial costs associated with your Hero's Heart circle be equitably shared among members?

5. Do you or your son have any special needs that the circle should know about? For example, sensory sensitivities, allergies, dietary restrictions, reading/writing/learning needs, or physical/emotional/social considerations. Considering *The Hero's Heart* curriculum, are there any accommodations or modifications that need to be made? Is there anything else that you would like the circle of mothers to know about you or your son? In what ways might the circle best support your son's or your unique needs this year?

6. The Hero's Heart creates a circuit of energy with other mothers that amplifies the love, nurturing, guidance, and empowerment we offer our sons. From this experience, a community is born based on love and support, on giving and receiving. How will your circle foster true community and maintain the connection with one another between circle gatherings?

7. What does our Affirmation, "*I Am Co-Creating,*" mean to you?

Integrated Activity

What He Needs Right Now

This integrated activity takes mothers directly to the heart of their hero-sons' needs at this time and encourages them to set their highest intentions for this circle experience. Mothers will get to know each others' sons and begin to develop or deepen the feelings of love and investment for each boy.

SUPPLIES

Prior to circle, each mother should select one or two photographs of her son that reflect his true spirit and bring them to circle. The chosen photos can be current or from his younger years. Place them on the central altar.

INSTRUCTIONS

Slowly and gently, read the following guided meditation aloud to the circle.

Close your eyes, begin to follow your breath, and let your body, mind, and spirit deeply relax. With your inner vision, slowly bring your son's face into focus. Recall your son's smile, and remember a moment you shared with him that was pure joy for the two of you.

In your mind's eye, take your son's hands and feel the weight of his fingers as they interlock with yours. Look deeply into your son's eyes now, the windows to his soul. See the varying flecks of color and the nuanced shades of light that make up your son's unique eyes. Your son's eyes are the same size today as they were on the day of his precious, miraculous birth. You have looked into these eyes for years, and you will continue for many, many years to come.

Now travel back in time, to that first moment when you truly looked into your son's eyes. Remember the moment you first saw him. Let the memory of that moment wash over you now.

Now gently let time progress in your mind's eye and hear the first words he uttered as a baby… see the first steps he took on his own…now, watch him walk into kindergarten for the first time, and gently, like flipping through the pages of a book, continue watching your beloved son as his life progresses year by year by year. Watch as his interests change, his passions develop, watch as people and experiences come and go. Notice what is changing and what is staying the same.

Imagine now that seventy years have passed and you are once again looking into the eyes of your son. He's now an old man, fully grown with a lifetime behind him, but still your little boy. The skin around his eyes is different now of course, but the eyes themselves? They have not changed a bit. Look deep into those eyes and see your son's heart. Recognize that he has been on his own path, his own journey, all along. Take a deep breath now, and listen to your son's heart. What is it telling you? You may ask him anything you wish. You may share with him anything you wish. Have a moment here with your grown son.

When you are ready, give him a kiss or a hug or whatever feels good to you, and slowly begin to see your son once again as he is today. He is in the middle of his boyhood, at the cusp of puberty. What does your son need in this chapter of his life? What does he need most from you as his mother right now? What miracles does your son need in his life? What miracles do you as his mother need in your life? How will sharing the Hero's Heart circle with your son and with this circle of other mothers and sons offer you these gifts? What hopes, dreams, and intentions do you have for this sacred year-long journey that we will be sharing together? What are your highest wishes for the Hero's Heart journey? I invite you to set these hopes, dreams, wishes, and intentions on our collective altar. See their manifestation in your mind's eye and give thanks for the blessings already on their way. And so it is.

Have another breath, beginning to feel the weight of your feet on the floor, of your body in your seat. Begin to wiggle your toes and fingers, coming fully back into your body and returning to the here and now. When you are ready, open your eyes and return to our circle.

Hold space for the mothers to share their response to and experience with the meditation. Invite mothers to pass around the photographs of their son and introduce their "hero" to the group. At this time, mothers may wish to share their intentions for this experience.

Quote Study

In and through community lies the salvation of the world.

M. Scott Peck

Never doubt that a small group of thoughtful committed citizens can change the world; indeed, it's the only thing that ever has.

Margaret Mead

....

Change will not come if we wait for some other person, or if we wait for some other time. We are the ones we've been waiting for. We are the change that we seek.

Barack Obama

....

The universe is no longer expanding in the same way. The frontiers our sons must cross are internal, not external.

Olga Silverstein

....

A tree stands strong not by its fruits or branches, but by the depths of its roots.

Anthony Liccione

....

When you teach your son, you teach your son's son.

The Talmud

....

An individual can't create anything itself. All of our dreams come true with the cooperation and co-creation of other souls.

Hina Hashmi

"I HAVE THE HEART OF A HERO"

❝ *Explore your heart, discover yourself, then give the best that is in you to your age and to your world. There are heroic possibilities waiting to be discovered in every person.* ❞
Wilferd A. Peterson

Dear Mothers,

Our sons are on a Hero's Journey. They are navigating a transformative passage from boyhood to manhood, which requires them to leave behind the well-known world of childhood and cross a threshold, filled with many challenges, into a new world where much is unknown. Along their journey, our boys need an abundance of real-life, positive role models – everyday heroes and heroines – to look to for guidance and inspiration. They also must begin to see *themselves* as heroes – the authors of their own lives, armed with the noble qualities and courage needed to complete their journey and arrive at manhood with integrity. This month, we will consider what it *truly* means to be a person of character – a *hero* – and then together, we will begin to open our eyes to the unsung heroism in ourselves, at home, at school, and in our communities.

What is the True Measure of a Hero?

Heroism should not be limited to stereotypes. Any program using the term "hero" as its thematic base must dedicate some initial time wrestling with the many stereotypes and pre-conceived ideas that pervade our culture. The "heroes" our sons encounter in the media and in popular culture are most often hyper-masculine archetypes: the warrior, the sports star, the wealthy celebrity, or the superhero. These individuals and characters are routinely depicted as very physically strong, dominating, invulnerable, tough, aggressive, isolated, promiscu-ous, competitive, extreme risk takers, and lacking emotional expression (aside from anger and vengeance). When boys are first asked to describe a hero, the words they choose almost always focus on physical acts, often with an interwoven thread of violence; heroism is rarely related to strength of character or peaceful solutions.

In circle this month, we will discuss the *actual* definition of 'hero' and reclaim its original meaning. Through this process, we will identify the noble qualities of a true hero, and work together with our sons to deconstruct the pervasive stereotypes and false impressions in order to reframe concepts of strength, courage, and heroism.

Son, Who Are Your Heroes?

During the highly impressionable period of adolescence children need good, healthy role models who demonstrate exemplary behavior. Boys (and girls) naturally seek out role models and examples for how they wish to live and grow, often following them with a passion. Dr. Alan Ravitz, a prominent child and adolescent psychologist at the Child Mind Institute in New York City, explains that, "as kids individualize themselves from their parents, which is a natural part of development and growing up, they try to establish psychological and emotional independence. No matter the culture, they need somebody to look to, aside from their parents, for guidance and a model for becoming an adult." In my first book, *The Heroines Club*, I discuss the lack of women's history taught in schools and the dearth of empowered female representation in popular culture, and what that means for our daughters as they seek to fulfill this universal and developmental need. I make the claim that in order for our daughters to "be it," they must first "see it," and then I offer a path for that vision. Here I am saying that although our sons' *gender* is certainly represented in every domain, a concerted, planned effort is needed to lead boys to role models that are healthy and honorable. Yes, our society offers boys ample gender representation, but the men in the spotlight do not necessarily embody the qualities our world most needs for the men of tomorrow to cultivate today. Our vital task as parents is to lead our boys to healthy, positive role models – people that personify our highest values and potentials as humans. We must not assume that our young sons can discriminate between healthy empowerment and toxic role-playing unaided. Just as with our daughters, if our sons are to be it, they must see it. And we must lead them to it. This month in circle, we will guide our sons to discover their own values and answer for themselves the questions *what does it mean to be a man of character, who is an appropriate role model for me, and who are my heroes?*

Son, *You* Are a Hero

During the outward search for guidance and role models, our growing sons are also turning inward, striving to become heroes themselves. They wish to live courageous lives, rich in honor and meaning; they dream of slaying dragons and giants, both literally and figuratively. Boys make actions and choose a path as if the hero instinct is buried deep in their DNA, and perhaps there is some truth in that idea. After all, in his theory of the human psyche, psychologist and founder of analytical psychology Carl Jung actually named 'hero' as one of the twelve primary archetypes that symbolize basic human motivation.

This month, we will empower the hero within our sons and harness their innate drive toward heroism for the greater good. Our sons will understand that each of them, already and just as they are, has the heart of a hero, and the dragon they must face is patriarchy's limited and toxic notion of masculinity. This is the central conflict today's boys must resolve in order to arrive at manhood healthy and whole. And to slay this dragon does indeed take great courage and nobility. It takes a hero.

We are in this together.

Love, *Melia*

Topic Introduction

Our Affirmation this month is: "*I Have the Heart of a Hero.*"

What comes to mind when you hear the word 'hero'? For many of us, we think of a man running into a burning building to save someone's life, or an extraordinary individual overcoming evil forces. There is often this sort of stereotype and false impression that heroes are make-believe, or exceptional people, endowed with superpowers. But that's not an accurate picture. Heroism is not reserved for the few, the special, or the elite among us. *Everyone* has a hero inside their heart.

By definition, a hero is: *a person admired for courage, noble qualities, and outstanding achievement.* During this month's circle, we will unpack these three concepts and see for ourselves that one's ability to be a hero has nothing to do with physical strength, age, gender, popularity, money, power, good looks, athletic ability, sexual prowess, exceptional talent, or material possessions. We will see that one's ability to be a hero has everything to do with what is in the *heart*.

The word 'hero' can also mean *role model*, as in, "who are your heroes?" Role models are people that inspire us by their example. They are people that we look up to and aspire to be like. Role models can come in all ages and sizes, and from all walks of life. They can be found in your home, in your family lineage, in your neighborhood, in your school, in your community, in your religious tradition, in history, and among brave activists and honorable politicians. We should choose our role models with thoughtful intention, for whom we admire shapes our perception of who we want to be. Through our circle discussion and Heartwork this month, you will choose your own hero. The story and example of this role model will provide you with learning, inspiration, and guidance as you grow and develop your own moral compass this year.

And finally, beloved sons, hear us when we say *your heart matters*. At this point in your life, a lot of time and energy is spent at school educating your mind, and in extracurricular activities, training your body. Try not to get confused and think that your mind and body are all that the world cares about or needs from you. You are a trinity – body, mind, *and* heart. As you grow into a young man, the courage and noble qualities in your heart will lead you to accomplish the outstanding achievements the world needs most. Now is the time to search within and cultivate the heart of a hero.

Discussion Prompts

1. What comes to mind when you hear the word 'hero'? What do you think it means to be a hero?

2. Must a hero be perfect? Can heroes cry, feel scared, or make mistakes? What personal characteristics would disqualify someone from achieving hero status in your opinion?

3. What are the differences between a hero and someone who is an idol or celebrity?

4. Courage is a core part of the definition of 'hero.' There are many different types of courage beyond simply physical bravery. What are some ways you are courageous? When is a time you have shown courage?

5. What relationship do you see between courage, noble qualities, and outstanding achievements?

6. What do you think is meant by the old saying, "heroes aren't born, they are made?"

7. What does this month's Affirmation, "*I Have the Heart of a Hero*," mean to you? In the coming month, what opportunity might you have to put this Affirmation into practice? What are some challenges you might face in practicing this month's Affirmation?

Integrated Activities

The Heart of a Hero

What is meant by "noble qualities?" This integrated activity provides our sons with an explicit and clear discussion of the morals, values, and traits of a hero. Through the activity, our sons will come to understand that by cultivating these noble qualities within themselves, they develop and strengthen their own hero's heart.

SUPPLIES

- Dry-erase board
- Dry-erase marker

INSTRUCTIONS

1. Using the dry-erase board and marker, draw a large heart shape. Explain to the circle that throughout the ages, the heart symbol has been a metaphor for the core of the self.

2. Aloud as a circle, brainstorm the noble qualities and positive character traits one might find in the "heart" of a hero. Write the words and phrases inside the heart. If the circle needs prompting, offer words and phrases such as *courageous, honest, kind, caring, champion of the oppressed, justice seeking, forgiving, resilient, altruistic, reliable, servant to those in need, sensitive, assertive, protecting, creative, selfless, confident, empathetic, patient, supportive, persistent, virtuous, passionate, thoughtful, generous, compassionate, autonomous,* and *connected.*

3. Once complete, take a moment to review the "Heart of a Hero" and ask the following questions:

- *Do these noble qualities require a certain body type or level of physical strength or size? (No.)*

- *Do these noble qualities require a certain gender? (No.)*

- *Do these noble qualities require popularity among peers? (No.)*

- *Do these noble qualities require a certain amount of money or possessions? (No.)*

- *Can anyone cultivate and possess these noble qualities? (Yes!)*

Soap Carving

Soap carving is a fun and easy way to create sculptures from a bar of soap. Your circle will carve hearts out of soap to serve as a tangible reminder of this month's Affirmation.

- Ivory soap bars (Any brand will do, but the soft consistency of Ivory soap bars seems to work best. Provide one for each circle participant.)
- Black markers
- Carving tools (carving or paring knives, butter knives, spoons, plastic knives, popsicle sticks, etc.)
- Toothpicks
- Bowl of water

1. Using the marker, draw an outline of a large heart on one side of the soap.

2. Using the carving tools, carefully remove the soap outside of the outline, making sure to remove small portions and slivers at a time. Cutting off too much at once will cause the soap to break off into chunks.

3. After the heart outline has been carved, use the toothpick to inscribe the word '*Hero*' in the middle of the heart.

4. Once complete, dip your finger in the water and gently rub the surface and edges of the soap to create a smooth finish.

5. Allow the carving to dry and harden.

6. To serve as a visual reminder of this month's Affirmation, enjoy using your soap or display it on your Hero's Heart altar at home.

Quote Study

I think a hero is any person really intent on making this world a better place.

Maya Angelou

....

Heroes are heroes because they have heroic behavior, not because they won or lost.

Nassim Nicholas Taleb

....

I think a hero is an ordinary person who finds the strength to persevere and endure in spite of overwhelming obstacles.

Christopher Reeve

....

Heroes become heroes flaws and all. You don't have to be perfect to fulfill your dream.

Peter McWilliams

....

No one was ever named 'hero' for following the crowd. Heroes set their own course.

Jonathan Lockwood Huie

....

True heroism is remarkably sober, very undramatic. It is not the urge to surpass all others at whatever cost, but the urge to serve others at whatever cost.

Arthur Ashe

Not the glittering weapon that fights the fight, but rather the hero's heart.

Proverb

....

It takes courage to grow up and become who you really are.

e.e. cummings

....

You are the hero of your own story.

Joseph Campbell

....

Watch over your heart with all diligence, for from it flows the springs of life.

The Bible

....

Few of us will do the spectacular deeds of heroism that spread themselves across the pages of our newspapers in big black headlines. But we can all be heroic in the little things of everyday life. We can do the helpful things, say the kind words, meet our difficulties with courage and high hearts, stand up for the right when the cost is high, keep our word even though it means sacrifice, be a giver instead of a destroyer. Often this quiet, humble heroism is the greatest heroism of all.

Wilferd A. Peterson

....

Fear and courage are brothers.

Proverb

There is no need to be ashamed of tears, for tears bear witness that a man has the greatest of courage, the courage to suffer.

Victor E. Frankl

....

Courage does not always roar. Sometimes courage is the quiet voice at the end of the day saying, 'I will try again tomorrow.'

Mary Anne Radmacher

Heartwork

MOTHERS

- Look for examples of everyday heroism and share them with your son.

- Notice your son's acts of courage, dedication to his goals, and noble qualities, and point them out to him with praise!

- Support your son in selecting, researching, and getting to know a personal hero. Help him to discover and articulate what it is about that person that he admires.

SONS

- Designate a special location in your room or elsewhere in your home, such as a bedside table or shelf, to serve as your personal Hero's Heart altar space. Place your Journey Journal and creations from each month's Integrated Activities and Heartwork there. When you look at your altar and the items held there, you will remember all we are learning and sharing in circle this year.

- Start a dialogue with at least three other family members and friends, asking them who their heroes and heroines are and why.

- Choose a hero (role model) to research and get to know this month. As discussed in circle, there are many ways to be a hero. The hero you choose can be any age or gender, and from any time period. Your person can be anyone that you feel fits the definition of a hero. Research your hero and place a photograph of them on your Hero's Heart altar.

"I CHOOSE RESILIENCE"

> *Every hero's journey is a tale at the intersection of fate and choice; while we cannot control the former, we can take full advantage of, and heartily relish, the latter.*
> **Brett and Kate McKay,** *The Art of Manliness*

Dear Mothers,

At the heart of the hero's journey lies the concept of being the hero of one's own life – of assuming a personal responsibility for the wellness and prosperity of self and community. A hero's development includes recognizing the adaptive potential of choosing how to react to stressful situations. The way we accomplish this in the face of adversity is through cultivating, and consciously choosing, *resilience*.

The word 'resilience' comes from the Latin word for 'to bounce back' (*resilire*). It is defined as the capacity to recover from difficulties and to adapt successfully in the face of threats, fear, disasters, stress, and overload. Resilience is our ability to persevere and adjust in times of adversity. A resilient spirit is one of the greatest gifts we can give our sons.

All children will experience times of adversity, and trauma is an inescapable fact of life. Trauma can result from events that are clearly extraordinary, such as violence, molestation, natural disaster, terrorism, serious illness, medical emergency, or the unexpected death of a loved one. But children can also experience trauma from common, ordinary events like changing schools, changing neighborhoods, not making the team, encountering bullies, medical procedures, and divorce. Even without the more consequential traumas, the adolescent years can be an especially difficult time for children as they struggle to meet extra academic demands and contend with new social challenges. A child with a very low level of resilience may respond to these unavoidable life traumas and adversities by manifesting aggression, depression, maladaptive coping strategies such as substance abuse and antisocial behavior, or even suicide. Children with high levels of resilience seem to "bounce back" from the bumps and bruises of life, and they meet challenges and pressures with confidence and perseverance. How our sons approach adversity and trauma, both minor and major, will have a massive impact on their overall health, happiness, and personal success.

Thankfully, psychologists and social scientists inform us that resilience is a skill to which we all have access – it is not a trait that people simply have or do not have. Instead, resilience involves *vital protective factors* – behaviors, thoughts, and actions – that may be learned, developed, and fostered.

The American Psychological Association reports the seven vital factors that contribute to resilience are:

1. At least one stable and committed relationship with a supportive parent, caregiver, or other adult.

2. Positive self-esteem and confidence in one's strengths and abilities.

3. The capacity to manage and regulate strong emotions.

4. Strong communication and interpersonal skills.

5. The tendency to look for positive meaning in one's life.

6. Maintaining a positive outlook.

7. Practicing gratitude.

Boys and Resilience

Consciously building resilience within boys is a vitally important matter. When we examine resilience through the context of gender, we see that boys are particularly at risk. As discussed in Part I of this book, as a culture, we generally groom our sons to be stoic, emotionally disconnected, and non-communicative. Although boys and girls are born with an equal sensitivity to emotions and an equal proclivity for expressive communication, boys are directed away from developing these skills and behaviors from the beginning of their lives.

For example, a 2014 study in the scientific journal *Pediatrics* found that mothers interacted vocally more often with their infant daughters than they did with their infant sons. In another study (*Frontiers in Psychology*, 2013), a team of British researchers found that Spanish mothers were more likely to use emotional words and emotional topics when speaking with their four-year-old daughters than with their four-year-old sons. Moreover, a 2017 study (*American Psychological Association*) from Emory University found that fathers smile and sing more to their daughters, and they acknowledge their sadness far more than they do with their sons. These researchers also found that the words fathers use with sons are more focused on achievement, such as "win" and "proud." Additionally, a 2015 study (*Journal of Pediatric Psychology*) found that parents use "directives" when teaching their two to four-year-old sons how to climb down a playground pole, but when teaching daughters, they offer extensive "explanations."

The spoken and unspoken patriarchal maxims of "how to raise a boy" and "acceptable masculinity" that infiltrate our lives are directly opposed to two of the vital factors necessary for resilience – emotional intelligence and communication skills. The influence of male gender stereotypes clearly places boys at a distinct disadvantage. *The Hero's Heart* works to counteract this negative influence and explicitly develop in our boys all the vital factors needed for lifelong resilience. Overall, *The Hero's Heart* is designed to nurture your mother-son relationship and support your son in developing a positive self-esteem and confidence. In Month 4, you will explore emotional intelligence and expression. In Month 5, you will consider the requirements for healthy interpersonal relationships and discover ways to nurture and maintain friendships. In Month 6 and Month 7, you will guide your son to develop and practice his communication abilities. And in Month 12, you will encourage your son to seek positive meaning and purpose for his life. As you can see, the book you are holding in your hands is a recipe for resilience!

This month, then, our intention is to offer our young heroes a potent dose of two vital factors needed for lifelong resilience in the face of adversity: *gratitude* and a *positive attitude*.

Gratitude

Resilient people observe and appreciate the little, positive things in life, and they find enrichment in the places that others might easily overlook. Resilience requires making a choice to be grateful, despite the situation. It means asking yourself, "*What can I be grateful for right now?*" During times of adversity and struggle, thoughts of gratitude have an amazing power to lift our spirits and help us focus on what is still whole and enjoyable in life, all the while flooding our bodies with endorphins – the "feel good" hormones. In over a hundred studies to date, researchers have concluded that people with a daily practice of gratitude consistently experience more positive emotions and demonstrate psychological resilience. Learning to practice gratitude is one of life's most valuable lessons, and this month we set the intention to offer this important daily practice to our sons.

Positive Attitude

Research shows that seeing the positive side of life's experiences and practicing positive thoughts lead to happier and healthier children and adults. A positive attitude is a vital factor for resilience, but we are not talking about a 'Pollyanna' approach to life or adversity. Positive thinking does not mean we revert to denial, or that we never experience pain and sadness. Instead, striving to maintain a positive attitude is about looking at the situation realistically, searching for ways we can improve the situation, and trying to learn from our experiences.

In her book *Positivity*, social psychology researcher Dr. Barbara Fredrickson noted, "resilient people are characterized by an ability to experience both negative and positive emotions, even in the face of difficult or painful situations. They mourn losses and endure frustrations, but they also find redeeming potential or value in most challenges. When not-so-resilient people face difficulties, all of their emotions turn negative. Resilient people, while they certainly see and acknowledge the bad, will find a way to also see the good." In other words, resilient people acknowledge the cloud, but they can also perceive a silver lining.

Whether or not this kind of approach to life comes naturally to your son, positive thinking is a skill that can be taught, learned, and cultivated at any age. This month, we will highlight for our sons the strong relationship between thoughts, feelings, and how we experience life.

Choice

While we cannot control much of what happens in the world, we can choose how we respond to the events that befall us. We can always choose our attitude and where to focus our mental energy.

Life can be harsh, even horrible at times, and the choices we make about how we respond are critical. Our sons lead rich, complex lives and they will experience failures, troubles, and obstacles to overcome. The moment they realize that they have a choice in the matter, they step into their power and onto the path of becoming the heroes of their own lives.

Resilience, Choice, and Victim Blaming

If we are going to talk about resilience and choice and being the hero of our own lives, I must make this clear: of course, there are times when people are truly victimized. Domestic violence, child abuse, rape, theft, war, terrorism, natural disaster, extreme poverty, and other disastrous circumstances are genuinely horrible things. We are not trivializing these painful and calamitous experiences. We are not blaming anyone for their circumstances or any harm that has befallen them. In theater work, it's called the "Yes, and…" approach. *Yes*, you have been a victim of your circumstance, *and* you are a hero for choosing resilience. What we are doing this month is seeking to empower the hero inside our sons' hearts, not discrediting any real victimhood.

I used to have a bumper sticker on my car that read, "We are all doing the best we can." When I think about life, trauma, choice, and resilience this is what I most feel: we are all doing the best we can, given the tools and resources we have, and the circumstances and situations we are experiencing. *There is no blame, only empowerment.*

I like to think of resilience as the amount of gas in your car. The more you have, the further you can go. This month we are going to help our sons build a reservoir of resilience within themselves and teach them to call upon that energy to contend with the challenges life throws their way.

We are in this together.

Love, *Melia*

Topic Introduction

Our Affirmation this month is: "*I Choose Resilience.*"

Heroes choose resilience. Resilience is the quality that helps us bounce back after experiencing adversity. It is the ability to face setbacks, failures, crises, and pain with confidence and courage. It is what helps us get up after we have fallen down, dust ourselves off, and get back in the saddle again.

Have you ever wondered why some people seem more resilient than others? For example, let's say Jeff and Marcos are students in the same seventh grade class. At different times during the school year, they both have run-ins with the same bully – another boy who teases and makes fun of them in front of others. When it happens to Jeff, he feels many negative emotions: anger, fear, sadness, and embarrassment. When it happens to Marcos, he too feels anger, fear, sadness, and embarrassment. However, a few days after the bullying incident, they diverge in their coping strategies. Marcos talks to a trusted adult, comes up with a plan for responding to the bully if it ever happens again, and commits to only surrounding himself with people that treat him with the kindness and respect he deserves. Meanwhile, Jeff tumbles into a downward spiral of negativity; he starts withdrawing from everyone around him, leaving himself feeling even more alone and isolated. Marcos and Jeff faced the same adversity, so why did one bounce back while the other did not?

You may have guessed that the difference lies in their genes – maybe Marcos was just born "stronger?" Or maybe it's the family circumstances? Maybe Marcos' parents are more supportive than Jeff's parents? Or maybe Marcos' family has more money and so he has more cool things to cheer him up? Even if those factors were true, one factor supersedes the influence of all the others when it comes to resilience. That factor is your attitude. Your attitude, the way you think or feel about things, has the greatest impact on how you experience life and how you recover from hard or painful experiences.

Believe it or not, your attitude is your choice. There are always multiple ways of looking at any situation and you get to choose where you want to focus your attention. If we set our mind to it, we can find misery in even the most wonderful circumstances and gratitude in even the most horrible.

"Oh, wow! You went to Disney World?!"

"Yeah, but the lines were so long, it was too hot, and my parents didn't buy me the souvenir I really wanted."

"Oh, wow. Your childhood home was destroyed in a flood and you were forced to move?"

"Yeah, but our friends, family, and community really supported us and we knew we were safe. Plus, I met a lot of great friends that I wouldn't have otherwise met if I hadn't had to move!"

Heroes know the importance of focusing on the good, because what we focus on we empower, and what we empower tends to grow bigger. Instead of looking for the bad in every situation, by looking at the good you have a chance to grow and learn from every experience.

We can't control everything that happens to us. We can't control the weather, where we were born, how others might treat us, our siblings' behavior, or what other people choose to do around us or to us. But there is one thing we can control: how we respond. We always have the choice of how we react. You always have a choice in how you think, what you say, and what you do.

Hardships and hard times are an unfortunate part of life. Sometimes bad things happen. Resilience is the hero's choice. This month in circle, we are going to explore the concept of resilience and how a daily practice of choosing gratitude and a positive attitude can help us when times are tough.

Discussion Prompts

1. Hard times can offer us many important lessons about ourselves, others, and life. Talk about when you learned an important lesson from going through a hard time.

2. How might counting our blessings during hard times improve our resilience?

3. One of the most powerful ways we can cultivate a positive attitude is by becoming aware of our "self-talk," the voice we hear in our heads. When it is negative, we can choose to stop it and replace it with a more positive voice. For example, if in art class, you notice your inner-voice saying, "I'm terrible at drawing pictures. I'll never be a good artist," you could replace it with positive messages of self-encouragement and self-motivation, such as, "I am improving with practice and I am proud of myself for sticking with it." What does your inner voice sound like? Are there any messages you wish to replace?

4. What are some ways you avoid or overcome a negative attitude when you can't control a negative environment or circumstance?

5. Do you believe resilience is a choice? Why or why not?

6. Who among your family, friends, and community exemplifies resilience?

7. What does this month's Affirmation, "*I Choose Resilience*," mean to you? In the coming month, what opportunity might you have to put this Affirmation into practice?

Integrated Activities

Stone in My Shoe

This activity illustrates the power of our attention and thoughts on our overall experience.

SUPPLIES

- One small stone for every participant
- Timer

INSTRUCTIONS

1. Each circle member will place one small stone in their shoe.

2. As a circle, you will take two five-minute, silent walks around the space, or outside if that is an option. For the first walk, instruct the circle to focus on the stone in their shoe – the way it feels, how it would feel without it, the way it impedes the experience, etc. For the second walk, instruct the circle to focus not on the stone, but on the beauty around them. If your attention is pulled toward the annoying stone, gently redirect your thoughts back toward the beauty around you.

3. After the two walks, remove the stones and place them on the altar. Allow time for each participant to share their experience with this activity. Was it difficult to focus on the beauty around you with the stone in your shoe? Were there things you missed in the first walk that you were able to see in the second? What did you learn from this activity?

4. Place the stones on the central altar for the duration of the circle. At the conclusion of circle, each circle participant will take their stone home to incorporate in this month's Heartwork activity.

Glass Slime

Glass shatters, but glass slime *bends* and bounces back! Enjoy making this satisfying glass slime that can be stretched, pulled, beaten, and shaped. Like us, glass slime is resilient!

SUPPLIES

(Per Circle Member)
- 1 five ounce bottle of clear glue
- Saline Solution (must contain boric acid and sodium borate)
- 1/2 cup water
- 1/2 teaspoon baking soda
- 1 fork
- 1 plastic Ziplock bag

INSTRUCTIONS

1. Empty glue into bowl.

2. Add ½ cup of water and mix the two ingredients together.

3. Add ½ teaspoon of baking soda to the mixture and stir. This helps the slime firm up a bit more.

4. Add one tablespoon of saline solution to the mixture. The slime will begin to form immediately.

5. Once the slime is pulling away from the sides and bottom of the bowl nicely, pick the slime up and knead it with your hands. Squirt a bit of saline solution on your hands to reduce stickiness as you knead your slime.

6. Place your slime in a Ziplock bag for storage when it's not being played with.

Quote Study

Life is 10% what happens to you and 90% how you react to it.

Charles R. Swindoll

....

In the long run, we shape our lives, and we shape ourselves. And the choices we make are our own responsibility.

Eleanor Roosevelt

....

I am not what happened to me, I am what I choose to become.

Carl Jung

....

Gratitude unlocks the fullness of life. It turns what we have into enough, and more. It turns denial into acceptance, chaos into order, and confusion into clarity. It can turn a meal into a feast, a house into a home, a stranger into a friend. Gratitude makes sense of our past, brings peace for today, and creates a vision for tomorrow.

Melody Beattie

....

We can complain because rose bushes have thorns, or rejoice because thorn bushes have roses.

Abraham Lincoln

....

So much has been given to me. I have no time to ponder that which has been denied.

Helen Keller

If you change the way you look at things, the things you look at change.

Wayne Dyer

....

The miracle of gratitude is that it shifts your perception to such an extent that it changes the world you see.

Robert Holden

....

Our greatest human freedom is that, despite whatever our physical situation in life may be, we can always choose our thoughts.

Victor Frankl

....

The greatest discovery of all time is that a person can change his future by merely changing his attitude.

Oprah Winfrey

....

The greatest day in your life and mine is when we take total responsibility for our attitudes. That's the day we truly grow up.

John C. Maxwell

....

You may not control all the events that happen to you, but you can decide not to be reduced by them.

Maya Angelou

Our lives are fashioned by our choices. First we make our choices. Then our choices make us.

Anne Frank

....

Between stimulus and response there is space. In that space is our power to choose our response. In our response lies our growth and freedom.

Victor Frankl

Heartwork

MOTHERS AND SONS

1. Listen to your inner self-talk and become aware of any negative, defeating statements that make you feel bad. Replace the negative statements by stating aloud or silently a positive Affirmation. For example, if you catch yourself saying "I am so bad at math! I'm never going to figure this out!" you might counteract and replace those words with: "With practice and help from my teacher, I am improving more and more." Remember, *you get to choose how you talk to yourself.*

2. Use your stone from circle to facilitate a daily gratitude practice this month. Lee Brower talks about a gratitude rock in the movie *The Secret*. In the movie, he placed a small rock in his pocket and decided that every time he touched it he would think of something for which he was grateful. You are encouraged to do the same this month! Keep your stone in your pocket or bag this month and whenever you see it or touch it, pause to think about at least one thing for which you are grateful. It may be something as small as the sun shining down on you in this moment, or something as large as having a family that loves you. At the end of each day, place your stone on your Hero's Heart altar, remembering the things you were grateful for that day. In the morning, as you return your stone to your pocket or bag, remember what you were grateful for yesterday. Over time, your stone will become a symbol, a physical object to which you can look to remind yourself of the many blessings in your life.

"I CHALLENGE GENDER STEREOTYPES AND DISCRIMINATION"

> *We've begun to raise daughters more like sons... but few have the courage to raise our sons more like our daughters.*
> **Gloria Steinem**

Dear Mothers,

As discussed in Part I of this book, one of the greatest challenges our growing sons face is overcoming the limitations placed on them by our society through toxic notions about what it means to "be a man." From infancy onward, boys are implicitly and explicitly pressured to conform to a prescribed idea of masculinity. From the moment they first hold a toy truck in their hands, they learn that society expects them to follow a rigid script of "appropriate maleness" and to demonstrate their masculinity with dominance, physical strength, and an absence of vulnerability. Our boys easily understand these societal cues, indeed they learn to read between the lines before they learn to read the lines themselves. They swiftly understand that in order to be accepted as boys, they must *prove* their masculinity, they must devalue within themselves any human traits generally associated with girls and women, such as emotional expression and empathy. By repressing healthy parts of themselves to meet society's gendered expectations, boys suffer from a hampered and impaired social and emotional development. And for the boys that do not, or cannot, meet gendered expectations, they often receive severe punishment from our society, becoming the target of ostracism and bullying. Thus, our beloved boys face an insoluble dilemma where they are damned if they do, and damned if they don't. We must hold space for another way.

To embody their full and unfettered selves – to give the world the best that they can offer – our boys, like our girls, must feel safe and empowered to be authentic to themselves. While our evolving society has become more aware of the damage gender stereotypes inflict on the female half of the population, the standards for men and boys are just as poisonous. We must demand the same rights and freedoms on behalf of our sons and men as we do for our daughters and ourselves.

One of the primary goals of *The Hero's Heart* is to raise boys with the awareness and skill to recognize, deconstruct, and challenge gender stereotypes. This month, you will foster reflection on the concepts of gender socialization, and gender inequalities. You will equip your son with the critical thinking skills to question gender stereotypes, critique gender representations in the media, and challenge gender discrimination in his everyday life. The concept of stereotypes will come up again and again throughout *The Hero's Heart* program as we engage issues such as feelings, friendships, communication, peacebuilding, body image, and sexual development. This month serves as a broad overview of all of the stereotypes facing young people today, and each will be further explored in depth in their respective months.

Renowned twentieth-century psychologist Erik H. Erikson, in his theory of the psychosocial development of human beings, described the adolescent's primary task as creating a stable sense of self and personal identity. This important time – this second decade of your son's life in which he is actively forming his identity – is a vital period to regularly talk about the impact of gendered expectations on his life's choices. A common phrase spoken in patriarchal culture is "boys will be boys," as if boys are innately destined to behave in limited, hyper-masculine ways. What I say to this is: *boys will be human*. We must support our sons to grow into men that are not trapped in a box of negative stereotypes. Indeed, many of the qualities associated with masculinity are positive and needed, such as courage and assertiveness. We seek to affirm and celebrate the healthy masculinity within our sons without upholding toxic stereotypes that establish many of the pathological ills troubling boys and men today. We seek to empower our sons to construct an identity that is not rooted in sexism, and free them to know that they do not have to relinquish any parts of their humanity to become "real" men.

We are in this together.

Love, *Melia*

Topic Introduction

To support the visual learners in your circle, I recommend you have the following definitions written on a large paper or markerboard for viewing:

<u>Sex</u>: a biological concept based on genetics, chromosomes, internal and external reproductive organs, and hormonal activity in the body. Male or female.

<u>Gender</u>: a cultural concept based on belief systems about how boys/men/masculinity and girls/women/femininity should present. Boy or girl.

<u>Masculinity</u>: the qualities/behaviors society generally associates with boys/men.

<u>Femininity</u>: the qualities/behaviors society generally associates with girls/women.

<u>Stereotype</u>: the expectations that all members of a group are similar, with no individual differences.

<u>Discrimination</u>: the unjust or prejudicial treatment of different categories of people.

Our Affirmation this month is: "*I Challenge Gender Stereotypes and Discrimination.*"

To open our topic this month, we will begin with an explanation of what these words mean, to be sure that we all have the same understanding and foundational knowledge. These concepts can be difficult to grasp, even for adults, so don't be afraid to ask questions until we all feel we have a good understanding.

In general terms, 'sex' refers to the biological differences between males and females determined at conception and recognized at birth, such as having a penis or vagina. Gender, on the other hand, refers to the culturally defined attitudes and behaviors associated with, and expected of, the two sexes. The male sex is associated with the masculine gender, and the female sex is associated with the feminine gender. Unlike your sex, your gender is not located within your body. Masculinity and femininity are not something you are born with. Instead, gender roles are social constructs, which means they are essentially "made up" by a culture. It also means they can be changed. In fact, gender expectations have shifted many times throughout history. Did you know that high heels, makeup, wigs, and the color pink were once primarily associated with masculinity and the "male" gender?

Our society tends to emphasize and exaggerate gender differences in the form of stereotypes, or assumptions about people based on their gender. Examples of gendered stereotypes include "all girls are good at reading" or "all boys like sports." This is a problem that our culture divides into categories the human qualities that we all have the ability to share. Gender stereotypes lead to gender discrimination. By this age, you are likely very aware of gender stereotypes, even if you hadn't yet realized that is what they are, or the impact they have on your behaviors and choices. This month, we are going to open our eyes to the stereotypes all around us. We will look at the common forms of stereotypes and discrimination both boys and girls are likely to face, and develop strategies to take responsibility and stand strong in the face of discrimination.

Our Affirmation this month has two important meanings, which can be differentiated by where we place the emphasis. One interpretation is "*I* challenge gender stereotypes and discrimination." As in, *I myself* am brave enough to be fully authentic and true to myself, even if that means stepping outside of the box and not matching the stereotypes society has for me as a boy. The interpretation shifts slightly when we place emphasis on the word *challenge*. As in, on behalf of my brothers and sisters of the world, I *challenge* gender stereotypes and discrimination; I *support* and *defend* everyone person's right to live outside the box of gender stereotypes.

Beloved sons, you are free to be exactly who you are. You define for yourselves what it means to you to be a boy, and soon, a man. We know that it takes courage to make decisions on how to look, act, and live based on your individual thoughts and feelings, rather than societal expectations. We know that it takes courage to speak up and take a stand for what is right in the face of gender discrimination. We also know that you can do these things, because you are a hero.

Discussion Prompts

1. In what ways are boys shamed when they do not act "masculine" enough or girls shamed when they do not act "feminine" enough?

2. Have you, or someone you know, ever faced gender stereotypes or discrimination when you were pursuing an interest that others did not support? How did you feel? How did you handle it? What did you learn from that experience?

3. Where do we learn gender stereotypes? In what ways are children taught gender stereotypes? How do people learn what it means to be a boy/man and a girl/woman?

4. Have you ever hidden a part of yourself (a thought, feeling, or interest) or pretended to be different than you really are to fit into gender stereotypes? How did that feel?

5. Have you ever heard the phrases "man up" or "be a man?" Or how about "like a girl," as in, "you throw like a girl?" What do these phrases mean to you? Are they empowering or are they limiting? How might you respond if someone ever says these to you or someone around you?

6. What would it take for boys to feel free to value and express their full humanity? What kinds of changes would you like to see at your school and in your community? How can you help create those changes?

7. What does this month's Affirmation, "*I Challenge Gender Stereotypes and Discrimination*," mean to you? In the coming month, what opportunities will you have to practice this Affirmation? What are some challenges you might face in practicing this month's Affirmation?

Integrated Activities

Thinking Outside the Gender Box

A first step to overcoming stereotyped thinking is to be aware of what stereotypes people hold.

SUPPLIES

- Large dry-erase board
- Marker
- Eraser

INSTRUCTIONS

1. Remind the circle of the definitions for gender and stereotype, and explain that for this activity, you will be exploring stereotypes based on gender.

2. On the dry-erase board, draw two large boxes, one representing "girl" stereotypes and one representing "boy" stereotypes.

3. Beginning with the "boy" box, ask the circle the following questions and write their words or phrases in the box.

- *What are some stereotypes about how boys behave?*
- *What are some stereotypes about what boys like and dislike?*
- *What are some stereotypes about how boys look/think/feel?*
- *What are some stereotypes about what boys are good at and not good at?*

   (Examples are: plays video games, enjoys outdoor activities, good at math and science, likes sports, never cries, likes cars, physically strong, athletic, good at fixing things, likes to get dirty, loud, take out the garbage, wears jeans, most friends are boys, etc.)

4. Moving to the "girl" box, ask the circle the following questions and write their words or phrases in the box.

- *What are some stereotypes about how girls behave?*
- *What are some stereotypes about what girls like and dislike?*
- *What are some stereotypes about how girls look/think/feel?*
- *What are some stereotypes about what girls are good at and not good at?*

(Examples are: loves to shop, likes to draw and paint, wears makeup, has long hair, loves babies, emotional, likes to dance, pretty, likes dolls, wears dresses and skirts, likes the color pink, good at reading, quiet, helpless, most friends are girls, etc.)

5. Spend a moment looking at the two boxes. Remind the circle that these boxes include things that boys and girls are "supposed" to do or be like, not how they might actually be. Ask the circle:

- *When you look at these boxes, how do you feel?*
- *Are there any attributes that apply to every girl or every boy? (No.)*
- *Is there anything in the boy box that girls are not able to do? (No.)*
- *Is there anything in the girl box that boys are not able to do? (No.)*
- *What do boys/men have to give up to fit in the "boy" box? What do girls/women have to give up?*
- *What would happen if someone steps outside of his/her box or doesn't fit in his/her box? What words are used to describe these people? Are those words meant to be an insult?*
- *Why might boys or girls try to stay in his/her box even if they are uncomfortable there?*
- *What would make it safer for a boy or girl who can't or doesn't want to fit in the box to openly live outside the box?*

Remind the circle that while some people may generally fit a gender stereotype more than others, almost everyone sometimes feels "outside the box," and that while most people's gender identity (the sense of being a girl or a boy) aligns with their biological sex, for some people, gender identity is not so clear, and the sense of being "other," "both," or "neither" best describes their reality – and that too is perfectly okay.

6. To avoid reinforcing the stereotypes (rather than subverting them), it is necessary to end with a discussion. Erase the boxes, leaving only the words and phrases, to demonstrate equality. Explain that each person has individual desires, thoughts, and feelings, regardless of their gender, and that we have a right to be exactly who we are. We don't have to accept the limitations of stereotypes; we have the power to decide what makes sense for us!

The Mask You Live In viewing and discussion

Maria Shriver teamed up with The Representation Project in 2015 to create the documentary *The Mask You Live In*. This moving documentary follows boys and young men as they struggle to stay true to themselves while negotiating America's narrow definition of masculinity.

It is a film that actively seeks to change the conversation about what it means to display a "healthy masculinity," and as such, should be required viewing for every boy and man, as well as everyone who loves boys and men. Pop some popcorn and host a screening for your circle! The film is available for rent or purchase online. I recommend the "Youth Version" of the movie, which is available through the film's website: **https://tinyurl.com/z6xqcg7**

Quote Study

Gender equality is critical to the development and peace of every nation.

Kofi Annan

....

The problem with gender is that it prescribes how we should be, rather than recognizing how we are.

Chimamanda Ngozi Adichie

....

The soul has no gender.

Clarissa Pinkola Estés

....

A feminist is anyone who recognizes the equality and full humanity of women and men.

Gloria Steinem

....

A man is not determined by how much he earns. You can still be the man of the house and earn less than your woman. Being a man is not what you have, it's who you are. Being more of a man doesn't mean your woman has to be less than you.

Trevor Noah

School is very conformist, and one of the very first conforming that goes on in preschool and kindergarten is gender.

Dan Savage

....

Stereotypes lose their power when the world is found to be more complex than the stereotype would suggest. When we learn that individuals do not fit the group stereotype, then it begins to fall apart.

Ed Koch

....

I'm not ashamed to dress 'like a woman' because I don't think it's shameful to be a woman.

Iggy Pop

....

He wears a mask, and his face grows to fit it.

George Orwell

....

Tear off the mask. Your face is glorious.

Rumi

....

Gender equality is the unfinished business of the 21st century.

Hillary Clinton

Both men and women should feel free to be sensitive. Both men and women should feel free to be strong. It is time that we all perceive gender on a spectrum, not as two opposing sets of ideals.

Emma Watson

....

When you label somebody and put them in a box, then you put the lid on the box, and you just never look inside again. I think it's much more interesting for human beings to look at each other's stories and see each other. Really see each other and then see themselves through other people's stories. That's where you start to break down stereotypes.

Stephanie Beatriz

....

What upset grownups of both sexes about Elvis' performance was that he had broken the deepest taboo of all. He used his body as rhythmically and erotically and seductively as a woman – that was the forbidden territory he had entered. It was not only repulsive and offensive – it was nauseating – the word most used. It was an attack on male dignity. The kids, however, not yet grown into the stereotypes of gender, saw in him an exhilarating physical freedom.

Elaine Dundy

Heartwork

MOTHERS AND SONS

The media have a tremendous impact on how we are socialized and what we are taught about what it means to be a boy or a girl. Unfortunately, gender stereotypes in media are the rule, not the exception. Recognizing the stereotypes embedded in media is the first step to overcoming them. This month, as you listen to music, watch television shows and movies, play video games, see commercials, or read magazines, pay conscious attention to the way the media represent boys/men and girls/women. Point out stereotypes to one another and discuss them.

What gender stereotypes do you see or hear? What do you notice? How do these stereotypes oppress people? How do you feel about them?

"I EXPRESS MY
FEELINGS IN HEALTHY WAYS"

> *Patriarchal mores teach a form of emotional stoicism to men that says they are more manly if they do not feel, but if by chance they should feel and the feelings hurt, the manly response is to stuff them down, to forget about them, to hope they go away.*
> **bell hooks**

Dear Mothers,

At the time of this writing, hurricane season has reached the Atlantic. Hurricane Harvey created a catastrophic flood disaster in Texas, leaving whole cities essentially underwater. Many have died, and countless others have had their homes and lives upended. Just before sitting down to write this chapter, I saw a news interview of one such affected family. A grandmother stood speaking amidst the wreckage of their home, flanked on either side by her two teenage grandsons. The boys stood beside their grandmother like the Queen's Guard, solid and unflinching, as she recounted the calamity they had just survived. As the grandmother spoke, a contrast appeared between her tears and sobs and the complete silent stoicism of her two grandsons. At one point during the interview, the news anchor said, "You must be very proud of the two strong young men you have by your side. Men who clearly are holding it together for you. Boys, the strength you are showing right now will serve you your entire lives. You clearly have raised them to be fine young men." At these words, I swear I saw the young men's jaws clinch a little harder, and chins jut out a little farther, as they fought to hold steady the tender flood gates inside themselves.

As we learned last month through our study of gender stereotypes, one of the most devastating aspects of traditional male training is the pressure to not show any feelings. From very early on our sons are told in myriad ways that being emotionally open and honest equates to weakness, and that weakness is unacceptable. Boys are told to never show any sadness or vulnerability. Boys are told they don't cry. Through praise and punishment, boys become conditioned to hide the vast range and inmost depths of emotions they harbor inside themselves. Over time, they steadily lose the ability to even *identify* what they are feeling, much less describe their feelings. When boys follow the script of repressing their own feelings, they tend to become phobic of other boys' feelings, and in turn they become the oppressors of other boys who show their feelings, ensuring that cycle of emotional amputation continues among their peers. This emotional imprisonment exacts a tremendous toll on boys, eroding their mental health and the quality of their relationships. As we know, unexpressed feelings do not go away. Stifled emotions, swallowed tears, and inhibited needs manifest in other ways, such as substance abuse, eating disorders, poor school performance, bullying, perfectionism, relationship and intimacy problems, depression, anxiety, panic, and physical ailments. The panoply of suppressed feelings builds up into something destructive, eventually bursting out in the only socially sanctioned way for boys – through anger and violence toward self and others. The consequences of this pressurized system can be dire.

For most boys, adolescence marks the time when they begin to mask their feelings. Harvard psychology researchers Deborah David and Robert Brannon have conceived four "personas" to watch for in adolescent boys. The manifestations of these personas often indicate important underlying feelings are unexpressed. You may recognize some of these features in your own son.

1. The "sturdy oak" persona, who tries to never show any weakness.

2. The "give 'em hell" persona, who goes for big risks no matter what.

3. The "big wheel" persona, who focuses, almost obsessively, on being "cool."

4. The "I'm not a sissy" persona, who fears talking about feelings will brand him a "girl."

So, what do we do about this? How do we save our sons from becoming frozen behind a mask of feigned stoicism like so many generations of men before? As Jackson Katz, the creator of an education program entitled 'Mentors in Violence Prevention,' states, "We have a responsibility to our sons to break down the systems of emotional constriction that lead so many men to live lives of quiet desperation, and depression, and alcohol and substance abuse and all the other ways that men self-medicate themselves."

Breaking down the systems of emotional constriction begins with examining the limiting stereotypes placed on boys' emotional intelligence. As our sons' allies, we must explicitly teach them that it is normal and healthy to feel all of the emotions that they feel, that experiencing emotions does not make them less masculine, and that expressing their feelings is an important part of their self-care. This month in circle, you will pointedly teach your sons to express what they feel, when they feel it, and give them the language and skills to do so. In order to effect true change in the lives of your sons, you will purposefully address problematic feelings, and together explore a variety of healthy, empowering options for handling them.

Many experts now recognize that a person's level of emotional intelligence may be more important than their IQ, and is certainly a better correlation of success, quality of relationships, and overall contentment. One of the greatest gifts we can give our sons is the ability to recognize, accept, and productively express all of their feelings in healthy ways.

We are in this together.

Love, *Melia*

Topic Introduction

Our Affirmation this month is: "*I Express My Feelings in Healthy Ways.*"

Feelings are an important part of the human experience. But have you ever wondered why we have feelings? We must have emotions for a reason, right? Otherwise, why would they exist?

Psychologists believe we have feelings for two main reasons: feelings let us know about our needs and they motivate us to act to keep ourselves safe. As an example, when you experience the feeling of loneliness, this tells you of an unmet need for connection with others. Or, when you feel tired, you know you need to rest. Imagine you are crossing a busy intersection and a car speeds up toward you. Chances are, you will immediately experience a rush of fear and anxiety that will prompt you to jump back into safety. Or imagine you meet someone new and feel warm and expansive in your heart when you talk with that person. The pleasurable feelings will motivate you to connect with them even more. Our feelings carry valuable information. They are an important part of who we are, how we grow, and how we live.

Sometimes our feelings are uncomfortable or even painful. We all have difficult feelings that need to be worked through sometimes. Big feelings like sadness, frustration, anger, fear, and shame can be hard to contend with, but they are natural. Everyone – girls and boys alike – experiences weighty, roller coaster emotions at some point, especially during puberty. Sometimes the toughest thing about feelings is being brave enough to share them with others. As we learned last month in our discussion on gender stereotypes, talking about and showing feelings can be especially challenging for boys in our culture.

Do you recall some of the stereotypes we discussed last month that had to do with feelings? A common gender stereotype is that boys shouldn't cry or talk about feelings of sadness and fear. A lot of boys buy into this notion and feel embarrassed when they cry, or feel as if they have to feign toughness to demonstrate their manhood. Isn't it unfair that our culture tries to tell boys to hide a natural, needed, and healthy part of themselves?

The truth is, sharing your feelings is the best thing you can do! It is important to share your feelings with others so that they can help you and try to understand what you are going through. Even if nothing can be done to change the situation, you will feel better by confiding in someone you trust. Sometimes we can feel quite alone in this world, but when we open up, we realize we are not really so isolated. Sharing what's going on inside also helps us get closer to the people who care about us and who we care about. Besides, ignoring our feelings and trying to stuff them down doesn't work anyway. Feelings we hide don't just go away. Instead, they build up and come out in other ways that we don't necessarily mean for them to, like depression, explosive anger, or treating ourselves and others unkindly. When we talk about our feelings, they can materialize and begin to heal. It is so important that you allow yourself to show and share whatever feelings pass through you, without shame.

The first step to sharing your feelings is to identify what feelings you have. You can't talk about what is going on inside you if you don't know what's in there yourself. Making a list of your feelings can help. You can do this inside your head or by writing it out on paper, or even by drawing pictures. Once you know what you are feeling, you can pick someone you trust to talk with, and choose the time and place that would feel best. For example, is this something you want to talk about privately, or would it be okay to have your brothers and sisters around? If you think you might have trouble saying what is on your mind and heart, it might be helpful to write it down on paper. If the person doesn't understand what you mean right away, try explaining it a different way or give an example of what is concerning you, for example comparing your experience to a character's in a movie, TV show, or book. If there is something you need, or something you think might help make things better, say it. There is always help and support out there when you need it, and it is your task to let the people who love you know what is going on inside of you.

In addition to talking, there are many other healthy outlets to express your feelings. For example, journaling, art making, and exercise are all good ways to release your feelings and discharge built up emotional energy. In circle this month, our Integrated Activity will lead us to discover other helpful things we can do to express our feelings.

In the midst of a culture that tries to keep boys in a restrictive box of stereotypes, the courageous find ways to be open and vulnerable. It is brave to let your tears flow. You are neither weak nor deficient for experiencing feelings. You are healthy and whole and brave. When you have the courage to show your emotions, connect with others, ask for help, and speak your truth, you give others permission to do the same, and thereby break the cycle.

There is no man more powerful than one who is in touch with his feelings, who can laugh and love, cry and grieve. This is a truth you can depend on. Expressing your feelings is an important part of your self-care.

As the heroes of your own lives, you are learning to recognize your feelings and express them in ways that help you.

Discussion Prompts

1. Have you ever been confused about your feelings – as if you knew you were feeling a strong emotion, but you didn't know what, or you thought you were feeling one thing, when really, it was something else?

2. Let's talk about crying. Have you ever heard the phrase "having a good cry"? Crying is a wonderfully effective way to express our emotions because crying is catharsis. Scientists even believe that chemicals build up in the body during times of elevated stress, and crying is the body's way of ridding itself of these toxins. Crying is so good for us and everyone cries sometimes! What do you think about crying? Is it okay for boys and men to cry? When have you seen a man cry? How did that make you feel?

3. Let's talk about anger. Psychologists agree that most often, anger is a mask for feelings of fear and/or shame. Think back to a time when you have felt anger. What other feelings might you have also been feeling at the time?

4. The hormonal changes of puberty greatly influence the emotional system. The balance between testosterone and estrogen fluctuates, often causing feelings to shift very quickly, and overall feelings of crabbiness to increase. Even though our cultural stereotypes tell us that girls are moody and boys are not, the truth is that everyone – boys and girls alike – feels intense emotions, especially during puberty. Have you ever felt your emotions shift quickly like a roller coaster? Or have you felt grumpy when you weren't sure why? Have you noticed a change in your emotions that might be related to puberty?

5. Our closing benediction each month includes the line, "we are strong". What does it mean to be strong with regard to emotions?

6. When have you seen or heard a boy being bullied or mocked for expressing his emotions? What might you say or do if that ever happens again while you are around? What might you say or do if it happens to you?

7. What does this month's Affirmation, "*I Express My Feelings in Healthy Ways*," mean to you? In the coming month, what opportunity might you have to put this Affirmation into practice? What are some challenges you might face in putting this Affirmation into practice?

Integrated Activities

The Guest House

In his poem, *The Guest House*, 13th-century Persian poet, Islamic scholar, theologian, and Sufi mystic, Rumi, tells us that all feelings are valuable and that each feeling, no matter how messy or uncomfortable to experience, has something important to teach us.

THE GUEST HOUSE

This being human is a guest house.
Every morning a new arrival.
A joy, a depression, a meanness,
some momentary awareness comes
as an unexpected visitor.
Welcome and entertain them all!
Even if they are a crowd of sorrows,
who violently sweep your house
empty of its furniture,
still, treat each guest honorably.
He may be clearing you out
for some new delight.
The dark thought, the shame, the malice.
Meet them at the door laughing and invite them in.
Be grateful for whatever comes.
Because each has been sent
as a guide from beyond.

Rumi, translation by Coleman Barks

SUPPLIES

- One typed copy of the poem *The Guest House* for each circle member.
- Glue or tape.

INSTRUCTIONS

1. Affix your copies of The Guest House into your Journey Journals.

2. Read The Guest House aloud in circle and discuss the following questions:

- *Which "guest" is it especially hard for you to welcome into your "house"? Which "guest" is your favorite to invite in?*

- *What do you think Rumi means by "each has been sent as a guide from beyond?" How do our feelings and emotions teach and guide us?*

- *What do you think happens to a "guest" that is not permitted to stay for a visit? If we push them out and lock the door, where do they go?*

A Self-Portrait of Feelings and Expressions

This integrated activity offers the opportunity to creatively explore all the feelings we experience, as well as the many healthy ways we can express them.

SUPPLIES

- Template of a head, neck and shoulders drawn with permanent marker on thick, sturdy paper – one for every member of the circle.
- Plenty of black Sharpies or other permanent markers
- Chalk Pastels

INSTRUCTIONS

1. Using the chalk pastels provided, fill in your head and torso with color to represent feelings that you experience. Try to think of as many as you can. For example: happy, sad, joyful, cheerful, curious, embarrassed, disappointed, jealous, excited, fantastic, generous,

nervous, brave, friendly, shy, ignored, important, interested, lonely, confused, bored, surprised, proud, frustrated, impatient, silly, uncomfortable, stubborn, worried, satisfied, safe, relieved, peaceful, overwhelmed, loving, tense, calm. Consider how color choices might be used to represent different feelings. Notice how the pastel colors can be blended together with your finger to create a combined effect, representing how we sometimes experience more than one feeling at a time.

2. Using the markers provided, write words (or draw symbols and pictures) to represent healthy things you can do to express your feelings. For example: cry, talk to someone, paint, draw, write a story, write in your journal, yell, dance, sing, punch a pillow, jump up and down, smile and laugh, go for a walk, take a warm bubble bath, pray, meditate, etc. Write these words on your page around your colored head and torso.

3. After the allotted time is complete, clean the area and gather supplies. Hold space for each son and mother who wishes to share their creation and give voice to the feelings they experience and how they might express them.

Quote Study

If you want to have a life that is worth living, a life that expresses your deepest feelings and emotions and cares and dreams, you have to fight for it.

Alice Walker

....

Colors, like features, follow the changes of the emotions.

Pablo Picasso

....

The best way out is always through.

Robert Frost

Feelings come and go, like clouds on a windy day. Conscious breathing is my anchor.

Thích Nhat Hanh

....

One can be the master of what one does, but never of what one feels.

Gustave Flaubert

....

The more room you give yourself to express your true thoughts and feelings, the more room there is for your wisdom to emerge.

Marianne Williamson

....

Never apologize for showing your feelings. When you do, you are apologizing for the truth.

José N. Harris

....

Our feelings are our most genuine paths to knowledge.

Audre Lorde

....

These pains you feel are messengers. Listen to them.

Jalaluddin Rumi

....

Many of us spend our whole lives running from feeling with the mistaken belief that you cannot bear the pain. But you have already borne the pain. What you have not done is feel all you are beyond that pain.

Kahlil Gibran

Just keep going. No feeling is final.

Rainer Maria Rilke

....

We cannot heal what we cannot feel.

John Bradshaw

....

My painting carries with it the message of pain.

Frida Kahlo

....

Feelings can't be ignored, no matter how unjust or ungrateful they seem.

Anne Frank

Heartwork

MOTHERS

1. Check in with your son at least daily, and ask him about his inner world.

•   *How is your heart? What's going on inside you? How are you feeling? What other ways could you describe your feelings? How can you express your feelings constructively?*

SONS

1. Like anything, expressing our feelings in healthy ways takes practice. This month, practice noticing what you are feeling, talking about it with close friends and family, and choosing activities that might help. Write about your experiences in your Journey Journal.

2. As you watch T.V. shows and movies this month, notice any gender stereotypes related to feelings. Write the examples in your Journey Journal.

"I AM A
HEROIC FRIEND"

❝ No man is an island.

John Donne

Dear Mothers,

Friendships are an indispensable part of life. They boost happiness, reduce stress, improve self-confidence, and nurture self-worth. They help us cope in hard times, and they encourage us to be our best selves. But friendship is not simply a "feel good" issue. Neuroscientists, developmental psychologists, and health researchers all agree: humans need close friendships, and when they don't have them, there are serious physical and mental health consequences. Physician and researcher, Dr. Dean Ornish, explains the importance of friendships: "I am not aware of any other factor – not diet, not smoking, not exercise, not stress, not genetics, not drugs, not surgery – that has a greater impact on our incidence of illness and chance of premature death."

In a 2011 study, Cynthia Erdley, a psychology professor at the University of Maine, followed a cohort of 365 middle school students. Using self-reported questionnaires that measured peer acceptance, friendships, loneliness and academic engagement, researchers found that having at least one quality friendship served as a unique predictor of both psychological and academic performance. "Having one good friend is enough to protect against loneliness and to help bolster self-esteem and academic engagement," says Dr. Erdley. Adolescents without close friendships are at risk for depression, suicide, dropping out of or disengagement from school, unintended pregnancy, and gang membership.

Clearly, our sons thrive by developing close, loving friendships with other boys. Unfortunately, because of societal norms, our sons are at a distinct disadvantage with this crucial aspect of their lives. We see the impediment our boys face foreshadowed in the recent descriptive statistics of adult men, and in what psychologists are now referring to as a "crisis of connection" in their lives.

The Crisis of Connection

The number of a typical man's friends and confidants has been steadily dropping for decades, leading to greater isolation and loneliness. Research from the UK reveal an estimated eight million (35%) men feel lonely at least once a week, while for nearly three million (11%), it is a daily occurrence. At least one in ten men say they have no close friends at all. A study published by the American Sociology Review reported that, of all the people in America, adult men have the fewest friends. If a man does have a confidant, three-quarters of the time it is a woman, most likely his girlfriend, wife, or partner. Of the men that do have friendships with other men, they report low levels of emotional support, self-disclosure, and trust within those friendships.

Could it be that men just don't want or need close friendships in the ways that women do? That is not what the available evidence would suggest. Researchers from Perdue University asked men what they desire from their friendships, and they found that men are just as likely as women to say they want intimacy. When asked to describe what they mean by intimacy, men say the same thing as women: emotional support, disclosure, and having someone to take care of them. In other words, men desire intimate, supportive friendships with other men, but they aren't getting them. Why not?

Gender Stereotypes, Homophobia, and the Crisis of Connection

The foundation of friendship lies in closeness – emotional and physical closeness. To be a good friend, one must be willing to confess one's own insecurities, be kind to others, demonstrate empathy, and sometimes sacrifice one's self-interest. But "real men," patriarchy insists, are not supposed to do these things. They are supposed to be self-interested, competitive, non-emotional, strong (with no insecurities at all), and able to deal with their emotional problems without help. As early as preschool, boys receive the message that the embodiment of true manhood is the "lone cowboy": independent, detached, and emotionally stoic. Being a good friend, then, as well as needing a good friend, is associated with being girly, immature, or gay.

Sadly, we live in an anti-gay society that devalues the feminine, the consequences of which are terrible, for all boys and men, gay or straight. In American culture, the fear of homosexuality discourages boys and men from looking toward other boys and men to meet their natural human needs for closeness and affection. Instead, they are taught to replace friendship with romance, and to look only to girls and women for emotional care and nurturing. This imbalance is an unfair burden on girls and women and further deepens the void that only friendships can fill. In a six-year study of 736 middle-aged men, attachment to a single person (almost always a spouse) did not lower the health risks associated with friendlessness, whereas a strong social support network did.

In an effort to understand these cultural mandates and the implications for boys' friendships, developmental psychologist, Niobe Way conducted hundreds of interviews focused on friendships with black, Latino, white, and Asian American boys longitudinally over three decades. She found that boys in early and middle adolescence often *do* have intimate male friendships and explicitly link these relationships to their mental health. Yet, by late adolescence, boys report a starkly different attitude toward male friendships and they reveal feelings of loneliness and isolation.

One boy, Justin, said this in his first year of high school, when he was fourteen:

My best friend and I love each other... that's it... you have this thing that is deep, so deep, it's within you, you can't explain it. It's just a thing that you know that person is that person... I guess in life, sometimes two people can really, really understand each other and really have a trust, respect, and love for each other.

By his senior year, however, this is what he had to say in response to the same question about friendship:

My friends and I... we mostly joke around. It's not like really anything serious or whatever... I don't talk to nobody about serious stuff... I don't talk to nobody. I don't share my feelings really. Not that kind of person or whatever... It's just something that I don't do.

In her book, *Deep Secrets*, Way writes, "Between the ages of fourteen and sixteen, boys are getting stuck in the box. They become obsessed with proving their manhood and proving what they are not. They become torn between the desire to be expressive in friendship and the gender-stereotyped expectation that they be assertive and forceful, or silent and strong." By late adolescence, Way continues, "boys know that their close male friendships, and even their emotional acuity, put them at risk of being labeled girly, immature, or gay." Way concludes that by the time a boy reaches late adolescence, emotional isolation has become virtually reflexive, and gender stereotypes become a self-fulfilling prophecy.

What Can We Do?

The loneliness of late-adolescent boys and adult men must be addressed in the lives of younger boys. We must challenge these toxic stereotypes and strive to prevent them from taking root in our sons' hearts. We must give our boys the skills, permission, and encouragement to cultivate healthy friendships and meaningful connections with other boys. We must show and tell our sons that stepping into manhood does not require stepping into "the box."

Way found that the primary support for boys' abilities to build emotionally intimate male friendships, and thereby resist gender stereotypes, is in parents who offer them a safe environment to talk freely about their thoughts and feelings. Each month, as we gather in sacred circle together, we break the superficial dynamic between boys by establishing safety, building trust, and over time, sharing intimacy. By offering the positive experience of talking freely about their thoughts and feelings with other boys, we are offering our sons a blueprint for relating to others that says: emotional intimacy with other boys is normal and good.

Our goal this month is to help our boys understand the importance of close, loving friendships with other boys, and to explore together how they can establish and maintain those relationships. We aim to destigmatize help-seeking and emotional vulnerability in relationships, and to teach our sons that intimate friendships need not be defined by gender or sexual orientation; friendships are human. Finally, we will insist that our sons challenge homophobia within themselves and their peer groups, for it is only when we live in a society where all are valued, respected, and treated equally that all can be free.

We are in this together.

Love, *Melia*

Topic Introduction

Our Affirmation this month is: "*I Am a Heroic Friend.*"

Friendships are a core part of the human experience. Both girls and boys need close relationships in which they can talk about what is going on in their lives, share their feelings, and count on one another to be there for them. It is normal and healthy for you to desire close relationships with other boys. In fact, a researcher named Naomi Way interviewed hundreds of boys your age and almost all of them expressed deep love for their friends. She noticed something interesting, though. A few years later, when she asked those same boys about their friendships, rather than talking about their love, most of them downplayed their feelings or claimed they didn't have any close friends at all. Way concluded that the natural closeness boys feel for one another is pushed down or denied as they progress through high school in part because many boys are afraid of acting in a way that makes them be seen or thought of as girlish or gay. The boys that she interviewed mourn the loss intensely and they still grieve as adults. Since publishing her book, Way says she has been surprised by all the letters she has received from grown men telling her how much they miss their own boyhood friends. Isn't it a shame that gender stereotypes and homophobia (which is prejudice against homosexual people) have made it difficult for boys to connect with each other on a naturally emotional and physical level?

Over the past two months in circle, we have discussed gender stereotypes and the importance of challenging them. This month, we are going to consider the impact of friendships with other boys, and how those relationship might be hurt or restricted by homophobia and gender stereotypes. We are also going to discuss what characteristics are important in a friend, how to identify a good friend, and how to practice skills that help people develop close friendships. And finally, because we know that to have a good friend, one must be a good friend, we will explore what it really means to be a "heroic friend."

Together we have created a community of friendship and brotherhood where we practice the skills of true friendship. The authentic and caring ways we interact in circle can be a model for the way you interact with your male friends for the rest of your life. Heroes believe and honor the importance of developing and keeping close and loving friendships.

Discussion Prompts

1. Why do you think friendship is important? How do people become friends?

2. Have you noticed differences between girls' friendships and boys' friendships? How do girls express their feelings for one another? How do boys? What do you think might be the cause of the differences?

3. Homophobia is one of the last remaining types of discrimination our society still tolerates, and it is unacceptable. As heroes, our responsibility is to challenge homophobia when we see it. Where do you notice homophobia in the boys around you? How might you challenge homophobia when you witness it?

4. Is there a difference between popularity and friendship? Can someone be popular but not be a good friend? Is it better to have one good friend who you can truly be yourself around, or a large group of friends that you feel you must be fake around to be accepted? Why?

5. All friendships have their ups and downs. How do you handle it when you fight with a friend? How do you communicate anger, disappointment, frustration, or worry?

6. Boys' friendships often include a fair amount of teasing. What is the difference between friendly banter and unkind or cruel teasing?

7. What does this month's Affirmation, "*I Am a Heroic Friend*," mean to you? In the coming month, what opportunity might you have to put this Affirmation into practice? What are some challenges you might face in trying to do so?

Integrated Activities

Climbing Rope Friendship Bracelet

A powerful metaphor for the importance of healthy relationships in one's life is rock climbing. Mountain climbers use a technique called belaying, in which a rope connects two people, the climber and the belayer. As the climber ascends the mountain, the partner on the ground lets the rope out, creating just enough slack for the climber to advance. When the climber is not moving, the partner applies tension and pulls the rope taut. This allows that if a climber falls, he or she will not fall far. Essentially, the belayer holds the life of the climber in his hands. Mountain climbers depend on each other and they must be able to trust their friends at the other end of the rope. Like rock climbing, life requires good friends who will catch us when we fall and support us when we rise. This integrated activity illuminates the qualities of a good friend and serves as a symbolic reminder of this month's Affirmation.

SUPPLIES

- Spool of knotting cord
- Scissors

INSTRUCTIONS

1. The facilitator begins by holding the end of the cord in her left hand and wrapping the cord around her left wrist twice – once to symbolizing the importance of *being* a good friend, and once to symbolize the importance of *having* a good friend. As she wraps the cord, she will describe the attributes she looks for in a friend. She will then pass the spool of cord to the circle participant to her left, who will wrap the cord twice and share his response about the attributes he looks for in a friend, and so it goes all the way around the circle. Once the spool of cord has made its way around the circle, the facilitator will speak about the symbolism of the cord (the interconnection we share with one another, the importance of having and being a good friend, and how to know that someone is a good friend to you).

2. Carefully pass the scissors around the circle, allowing each member a turn to cut his/her string from the web and tie the ends together, making a bracelet. This bracelet will serve as a potent reminder of this month's Affirmation.

Lean On Me

Bill Withers is an American singer-songwriter and musician. His 1972 hit, 'Lean On Me', continues to be a well-known song today that reminds us that we all depend on each other, and that it is right to ask for help and support from your family, friends, and community in times of need.

SUPPLIES

- One printed copy of the lyrics to 'Lean On Me', which can be obtained online at **https://tinyurl.com/ybxepmro**

- A digital copy of 'Lean On Me' and a music player.

- Glue or tape.

- Pens – one for each participant.

INSTRUCTIONS

1. Participants affix their copies of the 'Lean On Me' lyrics into their Journey Journal with glue or tape.

2. As a circle, read over the lyrics together. Invite circle members to discuss a time when they needed someone (friend, parent, etc.) to lean on in order to get through a difficult time.

3. Listen to the song and enjoy singing along together!

4. Notice how at the end of the song, Bill Withers repeats the phrase 'call me' many times. Communication is an important part of any relationship. To support communication among circle members outside of meeting times, gather one another's contact information. Pass around your Journey Journals, inviting one another to write their phone numbers into each other's journals.

Reach Out to a Friend

Everyone loves to receive mail! There is something so powerful and personal, so real and tangible, in receiving a letter delivered the old-fashioned way. This Integrated Activity will allow participants to practice the fine art of letter writing and enjoy the pleasure of receiving mail from their Hero's Heart brothers and mothers.

SUPPLIES

- Envelopes – each participant should have one for each circle member, minus themselves. If your circle has 14 members (7 mother/son pairs), then each circle member needs 13 envelopes.

- Stamps – one for each envelope.

- Pens

INSTRUCTIONS

1. Each circle member will write their own name and mailing address on the middle of each of their envelopes (they will be the recipients of these letters.)

2. Place a postage stamp on the upper right-hand corner of each envelope.

3. Pass out your self-addressed, stamped envelopes to one another. Each member should receive one envelope from each participant.

4. Place your envelopes on your Hero's Heart altar. When you feel called to connect with someone from circle, take a few minutes to send that person a letter using the envelope they provided. Let them know you are thinking of them and wishing them a great day. You may wish to write about something you like or appreciate about that person, or describe a special moment the two of you shared that meant a lot to you. There is no right or wrong way to do this! The letters you write can be a couple of short sentences or take up a full page. You may wish to decorate your letter with drawings or stickers. Be sure to write your return address in the upper left-hand corner before mailing it.

Quote Study

A friend is one that knows you as you are, understands where you have been, accepts what you have become, and still, gently allows you to grow.

Unknown

....

Friendship is born at that moment when one person says to another: 'What! You too? I thought I was the only one.'

C.S. Lewis

Good fellowship and friendship are lasting, rational, and manly pleasures.

William Wycherley

....

There are no strangers here, only friends you haven't yet met.

William Butler Yeats

....

Friendship is the hardest thing in the world to explain. It's not something you learn in school. But if you haven't learned the meaning of friendship, you really haven't learned anything.

Muhammad Ali

....

The only way to have a friend is to be one.

Ralph Waldo Emerson

....

Have no friends not equal to yourself.

Confucius

....

A true friend knows your weaknesses but shows you your strengths; feels your fears but fortifies your faith; sees your anxieties but frees your spirit; recognizes your disabilities but emphasizes your possibilities.

William Arthur Ward

....

The better part of one's life consists of his friendships.

Abraham Lincoln

On the road between the homes of friends, grass does not grow.

Norwegian proverb

....

Isolation is the worst possible counselor.

Miguel de Unamuno

....

There is a difference between solitude and isolation. One is connected and one isn't. Solitude replenishes, isolation diminishes.

Henry Cloud

....

Friends can help each other. A true friend is someone who lets you have total freedom to be yourself – and especially to feel. Or, not feel. Whatever you happen to be feeling at the moment is fine with them. That's what real love amounts to – letting a person be what he really is.

Jim Morrison

....

Alone we can do so little; together we can do so much.

Helen Keller

Heartwork

MOTHERS AND SONS

1. Add 'Lean On Me' to your regular playlist and enjoy listening to it together.

2. Begin mailing letters to circle members.

3. As you watch movies and T.V. shows this month, notice how the male characters interact with one another. What stereotypes do you see being portrayed?

"I THINK FOR MYSELF AND TAKE A STAND FOR WHAT IS RIGHT"

❝ *This above all – to thine own self be true.*
William Shakespeare

Dear Mothers,

During adolescence, peers begin to play a major role in our sons' lives. Of course, the influence from peers can be positive and supportive, for example, in helping each other develop new skills, or stimulating interest in books, music, or extracurricular activities. However, peers can also have a negative influence, for example, in encouraging each other to skip class, steal, cheat, bully, use drugs or alcohol, and become involved in other risky behaviors. We know that "peer pressure" as a term is thrown around a lot in today's culture, and it might be easy to mentally gloss over it. However, the pressure from peers is real indeed, and something our sons will contend with, especially during their early adolescent years.

According to the American Academy of Child and Adolescent Psychology:

- 55% of teens with a substance abuse problem tried drugs or alcohol for the first time because they felt pressured from their friends.

- 70% of teens who smoke say they started smoking because their friends smoke or they felt peer pressure to try smoking.

- 23% of teen girls feel pressured to have sex.

- 33% of teen boys age 15–17 feel pressured to have sex.

- 19% of teens report they would give up using a mobile phone while driving if their friends agreed to do the same.

During this next decade of your son's life, he will be called to leave the relative safety of childhood and to confront a sometimes daunting array of social challenges. The choices he makes and the patterns he develops now can have lifelong impact and change the trajectory of his life forever. Our focus this month is to equip our sons with the skills to overcome negative peer pressure, to be an assertive "upstander," and to resist from the beginning getting involved in dangerous or inappropriate situations.

Why Peer Pressure Works

Humans naturally seek a sense of belonging and acceptance among their social groups. Belonging lies in the middle of Maslow's hierarchy of needs, directly after our basic physiological and safety needs. Because of this universal need to belong, which ratchets up in the teen years, the pressure from peers begins to exert a tremendous influence. "In early adolescence, everyone is kind of looking at everyone else and figuring out, 'Am I normal?'," explains Dr. Ellen Rome, Head of the Center for Adolescent Medicine at the Cleveland Clinic. "Kids in early adolescence often give in to peer pressure because they want to belong; they want to be liked and they worry that they may be left out or made fun of if they don't go along with the group," continues Rome. By late adolescence (around age nineteen), however, most teens have begun to establish their own identity, belief system, and place in the world, and as such, the influence of peers begins to wane. The early adolescent years – the season of life our sons are currently navigating – carry with them the greatest risk of self-destruction as a result of peer pressure.

The Power of the Pack

In her book, *Masterminds and Wingmen: Helping Our Boys Cope with Schoolyard Power, Locker-Room Tests, Girlfriends, and the New Rules of Boy World,* best-selling author Rosalind Wiseman presents a picture of how individual boys within a group operate in relation to each other. She notes that when adolescent boys gather to form a group, they tend to form a hierarchy. One boy emerges as the leader of the pack (these are usually, according to Wiseman, the boys that most closely match masculine gender stereotypes) and the others generally follow their lead.

When people are part of a group, they often experience deindividuation, or a loss of self-awareness. "Groups generate a sense of emotional excitement," writes Tamara Avant, Psychology program director at South University in Savannah, "which can lead to the provocation of behaviors that a person would not typically engage in alone. Think about the last sporting event or concert you attended. It is unlikely that you would have been yelling and singing the way you were if you were the only person doing it!" The group seems to make some behaviors acceptable that would not be acceptable otherwise.

When our sons are in groups of friends and peers, they must rely on self-confidence and personal convictions to make good choices, even if that means breaking with the pack. Our goal this month is to anchor a heroic sense of self so deeply in our sons' hearts that if the pack begins to head in a dangerous direction, our sons will follow the courage of their convictions and remain true to themselves.

Raising Upstanders

Raising our sons to resist negative peer pressure is not only for their benefit and well-being, but for others' as well. Our world needs more "upstanders," people who, when they recognize something is wrong, choose to act to make it right. We have a responsibility to our fellow brothers and sisters to raise sons who will speak up, act to intervene, or get help when things are not okay. In our sons' lifetimes, we cannot predict what situations will happen to them. Terrible things happen every day in our schools, communities, and world. While it is certainly upsetting to hear stories in the news of victimized people, perhaps even more disturbing are the stories that involve a group of bystanders standing by, passively observing, videotaping, even sharing online… but not acting to help those in need.

TRIGGER WARNING:
The following three paragraphs contain information about sexual assault and violence which may be triggering to survivors.

On July 9th, 2017 in Florida, a group of teenagers between ages fourteen and sixteen came across a thirty-four-year-old disabled man drowning in a pond. They recorded the man's struggles, but they did nothing to help. In the video of the recording, which the teens themselves shockingly posted on social media, the teens laugh and taunt the man as he slowly drowns.

On September 12, 2017, at a high school in Collingwood, Ontario, two boys ages fourteen and sixteen brutally beat another boy in the hallway at school. A video of the brutal attack, which was recorded by a bystander, shows the boy bleeding and lying on the floor of the hallway while the other students repeatedly punch and kick him. The victim's mother said her son was hospitalized with a concussion as a result of the brawl. "Somebody stood there and videoed it and that's horrific," the boy's mother said.

On January 7th, 2016, just down the road from where I sit writing this chapter, a fifteen-year-old girl was raped in the stairwell of our local high school, while school was in session. The victim went to the stairwell with three male schoolmates, but instead of "hanging out" as planned, she was raped by one of her so-called friends while the others did nothing to intervene.

How could these children stand by and do nothing?

Social scientists who study the Bystander Effect explain that speaking up isn't easy. In the face of strong negative peer pressure, the developmental need for belonging may even over-power the most basic human need for safety. Speaking up, intervening, or calling the police can be challenging when faced with the risk of ridicule or even personal injury. A recent study from Harvard, based on in-depth interviews with twenty-three middle school students, showed that respondents supported the idea of being an "upstander" rather than a passive bystander. But, "half of them acknowledged that in practice they often laugh when they see others victimizing peers in school."

As mothers, we must ensure that our sons know, and firmly believe, they have the power *and the responsibility* to positively impact the lives of those in need around them. We are called to raise sons who will stand up for what is right and intervene on behalf of others in need, even when that means going against the pack.

As you can see, this issue of peer pressure can be vitally important in a literal sense. This topic may feel heavy, and the task we are charged with may seem daunting, but we can do this, and the place to start is always with education and open communication.

We are in this together.

Love, *Melia*

Topic Introduction

Our Affirmation this month is, "*I Think for Myself and Take a Stand for What is Right.*"

As you continue to grow older, you will begin dealing with peer pressure more and more frequently. No matter how wisely you choose your friends, or how well you think you know them, at some point you will have to make decisions that are difficult and could be unpopu-lar. This month's Affirmation means that we choose to make our decisions based on our own inner guidance system, even in the face of peer pressure. It also means that when we are in situations where we do not feel comfortable with what is happening, we act with courage to intervene and speak up. Rather than laughing along, or silently taking no action, heroes choose to take a stand against wrongdoing. And who knows, you may even be a positive influence on other peers who feel the same way. Often it takes just one person to speak out or take a different action to change a situation for the better. Your friends may follow you if you have the courage to do something different or refuse to go along with the group.

Experiencing pressure from peers can occur in various ways. Sometimes your friends may ask you to do things that you're not comfortable with. Sometimes it seems like everyone else is doing something, so you think about doing it to appear "normal." Sometimes, peer pressure makes us think about doing things we don't normally do just to fit in. Peer pressure works because we all want to be included and liked by others. This isn't a character flaw; it is fundamental to the human experience. We *all* want to feel a sense of belonging. We all want to feel accepted. But to make the right choices in life, our call to courage is to make decisions based on our *own* inner moral guidance systems – that inner part of us that helps us judge what is right and what is wrong – regardless of what everyone in the crowd may be doing.

It's not always easy to speak up and resist peer pressure. Sometimes it's really hard and scary. Sometimes it's unpopular. But it is always the hero's choice. Think of all the heroes and heroines we admire throughout history – Martin Luther King, Jr., Rosa Parks, Abraham Lincoln, Susan B. Anthony, Nelson Mandela, Miep Gies, Malala Yousafzai – every important social change throughout history happened because someone was brave enough to take a stand for what was right, even in the face of persecution.

So, how do we, as heroes, decide where to stand in a difficult situation? We check in with our own inner moral guidance system, we draw upon our internal reservoirs of courage, and we take a stand for what's right, even when that means standing independently.

Discussion Prompts

1. Everyone gives in to pressure at one time or another, like when a friend begs to borrow something you don't want to lend. Why do you think people sometimes do things that they really don't want to do?

2. The first step to overcoming negative peer pressure is to recognize when it is happening. What types of peer pressure are you facing, or have you faced, in your life? How did you handle it?

3. What are some of things your classmates or peers do that everyone follows? How does that make you feel when you observe when this happens?

4. Do you find it more difficult to speak your truth to friends or to people you don't know very well? Why might that be?

5. One powerful way to combat peer pressure in your life is through self-approval. Self-approval means that instead of searching for approval outside yourself, you learn to approve of yourself from within. Do you spend a lot of time thinking about what other people think of you? Why or why not?

6. The root of the word 'courage' is *cor*, the Latin word for heart. In one of its earliest forms, the word courage actually meant "to speak one's mind by telling all one's heart." Why do you think it takes moral courage, inner strength, and the heart of a hero to think for yourself and take a stand for what is right?

7. What does this month's Affirmation, "*I Think for Myself and Take a Stand for What is Right,*" mean to you? In the coming month, what opportunities will you have to practice this Affirmation? What are some challenges you might face in practicing this month's Affirmation?

Integrated Activities

The DomiNO Effect

Peer pressure is a lot like dominoes lined up. If we push the first domino, the pressure of it falling will cause the next domino to fall, and so on. When we face peer pressure, we have a choice: to be like one of the dominoes and just go with the flow and fall down too, or take a stand for what we know is right.

SUPPLIES

- Large bag of dominoes
- Tape, putty, or other strong adhesive

INSTRUCTIONS

Prior to circle, set up two long rows of dominoes on a flat surface. Place the dominoes close enough to one another so that the cascade effect will occur when the first domino is pushed over. In one of the two rows, choose a domino close to the middle of the line and secure it to the flat surface with tape or putty. Make sure that this domino is secured firmly enough that it will not fall over when pressured.

Explain to the circle how peer pressure can act like a domino effect: when we are faced with pressure, we can choose to go with the flow or stand our ground. Demonstrate the two choices by activating the rows of dominoes. When you face peer pressure, you have a choice to be like one of the dominos that just goes with the flow, or the one who thinks for yourself and takes a stand for what is right. Afterwards, hold space for discussion:

- The anchored domino stood firm, even when faced with pressure because it was anchored to the foundation. What values, morals, or beliefs anchor you and encourage you to stand strong in the face of peer pressure?

- Look at all of the dominoes that did not fall because of the one who stood strong. Peer pressure isn't always negative. Think of a time when a friend standing strong or doing the right thing pushed you to also do something good for yourself or to avoid something that would have been bad.

Following the discussion, you may wish to allow time for circle members to play with the dominoes and create their own domino line falls.

Peer Inventory

This Integrated Activity will invite circle members to consciously consider their current peer group and the influence they may have on their lives.

SUPPLIES

- Journey Journals
- Pens

INSTRUCTIONS

When you were a little kid, your parents usually chose your friends, putting you in playgroups or arranging playdates with certain children they knew and liked. Now that you're older, you decide who your friends are and what groups you spend time with.

Motivational speaker Jim Rohn famously said that "we are the average of the five people we spend the most time with." Of course, everyone is their own person, but there is truth to the fact that who we spend time with will have a great influence on who we become, for better or for worse. As the heroes of our own lives, it is vital that we spend time with uplifting friends who make good choices, whose values align with our own, and who bring out the best in us.

In your Journey Journal, number a single page one through five and then set your pen down and close your eyes. Have a deep, relaxing breath and take a moment to consider all the different peers you interact with these days. Remember, a peer is someone who belongs to the same age group or social group as you. Peers can be friends at school, neighbors that you spend time with often, cousins your age, other kids on teams you practice with regularly, and any others that you play with or work with. As you see all of these people in your mind's eye, select the five peers you think you spend the most time with or talk to the most often. Write the names of these five peers on the numbered list in your journal.

Spend some quiet time looking at the list you have written. Next, take a moment to consider each name individually, and ask yourself: what are the main qualities, traits, or feelings that describe this person? You may wish to write your thoughts next to the name, or just think about them.

Questions to consider: *Do their qualities match who you want to be or become? If it is true that we are the average of who we spend the most time with, do my peers elevate me or bring me down? Are there any changes that need to be made for my highest good? How might I be a positive influence on the peers around me?*

This activity is primarily for self-reflection, but as with all integrated activities, hold confidential space for anyone who would like to share how they are feeling and any insights that were gleaned. It may be helpful to explicitly advise the circle to not share these lists with anyone outside of the circle as it could lead to hurt feelings.

Quote Study

The opposite of a hero is not a villain; it's a bystander.

Matt Langdon

....

The ultimate measure of a man is not where he stands in moments of comfort and convenience, but where he stands at times of challenge and controversy.

Martin Luther King, Jr.

....

The world is a dangerous place, not because of those who do evil, but because of those who look on and do nothing.

Albert Einstein

....

It takes nothing to join the crowd. It takes everything to stand alone.

Hans F. Hansen

....

No is a complete sentence and so often we forget that. When we don't want to do something we can simply smile and say no. We don't have to explain ourselves, we can just say 'No.'

Susan Gregg

Deep down in the human spirit there is a reservoir of courage. It is always available, always waiting to be discovered.

Pema Chodron

....

The time is always right to do what is right.

Martin Luther King, Jr.

....

It's better to walk alone than with a crowd going in the wrong direction.

Diane Grane

....

Don't let the noise of others' opinions drown out your own inner voice.

Steve Jobs

....

You are the heroes. You are the heroes every day.

Miep Gies

....

Our lives begin to end the day we become silent about the things that matter.

Martin Luther King, Jr.

....

What is right is not always popular, and what is popular is not always right.

Albert Einstein

Do what's moral, not what's modeled. Don't take your cue from what is going on around you.

Andy Stanley

....

True belonging doesn't require you to change who you are; it requires you to be who you are.

Brené Brown

Heartwork

MOTHERS AND SONS

1. Role play together. Everyone will face peer pressure at some point. Sometimes the reason why people choose to do things they don't really want to do is because they aren't sure what to say or how to get out of the situation. What are some common peer pressure situations you might face at some point? What are some empowering or creative ways to face up to the influences without compromising your values?

2. Develop a code word or phrase to help your son get out of uncomfortable or dangerous situations without having to open himself up to any social ridicule. For example, a text or a phone call asking, "How's Aunt Mary?" calls for a response like, "she just got in town and needs to see you. I must come get you right now." Or texting the letter 'X' could communicate "I need help getting out of this situation." Practice using this communication at least once so that it can be instinctual when it is needed.

3. When we connect abstract ideas to reality, it makes a much bigger impact on our hearts and helps to integrate the message more effectively. Find one example of someone who you know (or a historical figure) who has withstood peer pressure and has done the right thing. Learn about this person's story and consider placing a photograph of them on your altar.

"I AM A PEACEBUILDER"

> *Peace demands the most heroic labor and the most difficult sacrifice. It demands greater heroism than war.*
> **Thomas Merton**

Dear Mothers,

It seems that every morning we wake up to a new story of violence in the news. As I write this chapter, the U.S. is gripped by the latest tragedy, one of the worst mass shootings in its history. In the hours and days since the unconscionable violence in Las Vegas, questions abound: Was the shooter a terrorist or a lone wolf? *Was the shooter mentally ill? Did the shooter have a political agenda?* A question we never ask: *Was the shooter a man?* The answer is almost always the same; men have committed 98% of all mass shootings in the U.S. This knowledge is so much a part of our mental landscape that we take it for granted.

The dynamics of violence are profoundly shaped by gender. All around the world, men are the primary perpetrators of violence and dramatic statistics confirm that boys, as a group, act with more aggression and violence than girls. Men comprise 95% of people convicted of homicide around the world, they are four times as likely as women to be the victims of homicide, and they are more likely to suffer violent deaths during conflict. Of all killings committed by juveniles, about 95% are committed by boys.

Despite the clear pattern suggesting a serious problem, our society tends to overlook male violence until a dramatic episode captivates public attention, like the most recent atrocity in Las Vegas. And yet, in the wake of such a tragedy, the media-driven conversation about the causes tends to focus on two main issues: gun availability and mental illness. What this leaves out, of course, is perhaps the most important factor: the gender of the perpetrators.

Men and boys are *not* naturally violent. It is wrong to assume men are hardwired to harm others, and propagating this notion fosters resentment and despondency among young men, creating a self-fulfilling prophecy. We are so accustomed to associating violence with boys and men that it is easy to attribute male behavior to supposed innate violent tendencies. It's easy to assume men – and angry young men in particular – are born with a natural propensity to violence that only takes a spark to ignite. But over half the population carries a Y chromosome, and only a small minority of those people exhibit violent behavior: not all men are violent, violence-prone, or accepting of violence as a way of resolving conflict or attaining power. Therefore, violence in boys and men cannot be solely a factor of biology. So, why are men and boys, as a group, more aggressive than women and girls?

Several theories have been proposed by social psychologists, with most focused on the evolutionary theory of nature (our genetic dispositions) and nurture (the way our environment shapes who we are).

In the *Neuropsychopharmacology* article, 'Nature and Nurture Predispose to Violent Behavior: Serotonergic Genes and Adverse Childhood Environment', the authors hypothesized that genetics as well as environmental factors influence human behavior. The researchers (Reif et.al, 2007) sought to distinguish between offensive and defensive aggression, hoping this would facilitate understanding of the neurobiological side of aggressive behavior. Early childhood environmental factors such as an unfavorable upbringing have proven to contribute to aggressive behavior in children, and this kind of childhood behavior is predictably followed by similarly aggressive and antisocial behavior in adulthood.

The case-control study included 184 adult men who were all Caucasian, and each was assigned to either a "violent crimes" or "non-violent crimes" group according to their histories. Violent crimes were considered homicide and physical injury, while non-violent crimes were things such as drug offenses and fraud. Variables such as age, history of drug addiction, history of personality disorder, adverse childhood environment as well as different genotypes were measured as risk factors for violent behavior. The results of the study indicated that genotype and adverse childhood environment both independently increased the risk for later in life violent behavior. Therefore, the cause of the disproportionate rate of violent behavior in males is likely to be related to both nature and nurture. If boys and men, as a group, are at higher risk for violent behavior, then there exists an urgency to take a hard look at the environment breeding the behavior – our society – and do whatever possible to change contributing factors.

If you are reading this book and sharing the Hero's Heart with your son, chances are great that peacebuilding is already a high value in your home. The boys engaging in this program are often already being raised to seek peaceful resolutions to their conflicts. However, like our previous chapters illuminated, male gender stereotypes actively work against many of our values and intentions for our sons. This is especially true for peacebuilding.

Patriarchal masculinity would teach us that violence is the best way for men to prove their strength and power, and it discourages them from releasing their feelings in other ways. From an early age, boys are taught to be tough and physical, and that violence is an acceptable response to emotional upset. While patriarchal masculinity is certainly not the sole cause of any particular conflict, gender roles and toxic notions of masculinity definitely fuel violence. The values of patriarchal masculinity, such as toughness, dominance, asserting power over others, repression of empathy, and extreme competitiveness, play a major role in criminal and domestic violence. Even boys raised in peaceful homes are at risk of turning to violence when faced with societal and peer pressures to substantiate their masculinity through dominance and violence.

The time has come to focus our attention on the connections between socially constructed gender norms and violence so that we may begin to explore ways of significantly reducing the incidence of male violence.

This month in circle, we will teach our sons that real heroes exhibit the courage to overcome toxic gender stereotypes and promote peace. We will give them the proven skills to defuse violent situations and resolve conflicts by expressing their feelings constructively and by using problem-solving techniques. We will emphasize compassion over aggression, and teach our sons to empathize, mediate, negotiate, and create peace.

Violence pervades our culture and impacts young people every day, from guns on the streets to bullying in our schools. Only when we teach our sons to recognize toxic gender stereotypes regarding male violence, and to think strategically about their options, will they be better able to take care of themselves and one another. As parents, we have a moral responsibility to raise our sons with the skills, courage, confidence, and compassion of a true peacebuilder.

We are in this together.

Love, *Melia*

Topic Introduction

Our Affirmation this month is: "*I Am a Peacebuilder.*"

As heroes, each of us is called to live as peacebuilding leaders with the courage to prevent violence and promote peace.

Conflict is a natural part of life and can lead to positive change. However, conflict can also lead to violence. Because people aren't perfect and relationships are sometimes messy, we all need to learn to better resolve conflict and prevent violence in our lives.

Conflicts are like escalators: they can go up and get worse, or go down and get better. Each action in a conflict contributes to the conflict worsening or resolving. Physical violence, name-calling, threats, bullying, teasing, and other forms of negative communication tend to escalate conflict. With positive communication, compassion, and problem-solving strategies, conflicts can be deescalated and resolved peacefully. In this way conflicts can become an opportunity for personal growth.

Conflicts are often rooted in a legitimate sense of anger at oppression or injustices. Peacebuilders don't brush their righteous anger under the rug. There is a huge difference between being a peace*keeper* and being a peace*builder*, and we should not confuse the two.

Peace*keepers* fret endlessly trying to keep tensions from rising and avoid conflict at all cost. They maintain the status quo and often trick themselves into pretending nothing is wrong.

Peace*builders*, on the other hand, allow tensions to surface and encourage disagreements to be aired and resolved. They harness the power of their principles in constructive ways and seek to address the root causes of their legitimate grievances through peaceful means while also working to change those factors.

It takes courage to be a peacebuilder.

By using conflict resolution tools and peacebuilding strategies, we can resolve disagreements without resorting to physical or emotional violence. In this month's circle, we are going to explore together some of the skills needed to assert ourselves in nonviolent ways.

Heroes know there are better ways than violence to stand up for themselves and what they believe in. One of life's valued skills is appropriately responding to and handling conflict, since our response is what often determines how a situation will end. We are learning to resolve conflict peacefully with courage.

Discussion Prompts

1. How do we define conflict? Does conflict have to be physical? What causes conflict?

2. Is conflict always a bad thing? Why or why not? In what ways might there be opportunity in conflict? Can you think of an example from your own life experiences?

3. Which behaviors are more likely to escalate conflict and which are more likely to lead to a peaceful resolution?

4. How do male gender stereotypes contribute to conflicts and violence? Why is it important to challenge these stereotypes and how might you do so?

5. An important part of nonviolent communication is active listening – the invaluable skill of focused communication. This means fully concentrating on what is being said rather than just passively 'hearing' the message of the speaker, or just thinking about what you want to say next when your turn comes. Why do you think active listening during conflicts is so important? What does active listening look like?

6. One of the most difficult, but also one of the most admirable and mature things you can do, is to reflect on your behavior and admit when you are wrong – to say to someone, "You are right. I'm sorry." Why might this be hard for us to do?

7. What does this month's Affirmation, "*I Am a Peacebuilder*," mean to you? In the coming month, what opportunity might you have to put this Affirmation into practice? What are some challenges you might face in practicing this month's Affirmation?

Integrated Activities

I-Statements

An "I-statement" is a conflict resolution tool for sharing one's feelings about a situation without judging, blaming, or accusing another person. They are also used to take ownership for one's feelings rather than implying that they are caused by another person. This Integrated Activity will offer circle participants an opportunity to practice this important peacebuilding skill.

SUPPLIES

Write or print the following statements onto individual pieces of paper – one for each circle member:

You knocked over our project and now it's ruined. You are so clumsy!

You went behind my back and told other people my secret! You are two-faced!

You are a liar. You told me you would help me with practice and you never showed up!

You need to turn that junk off! I can't do my work when you are over there listening to your stupid music.

You left your lunch all over the cafeteria table. You're a slob and I'm tired of getting in trouble because of you.

You think all these stupid jokes you tell are funny, but I hate them.

You need to watch where you're going! Every day you bump into me when you try to get to your locker and I'm tired of it!

You are driving me crazy by tapping your stupid pencil all the time.

There is no way I am working in a group with you again. Last time, you didn't help at all and I had to do all the work. You're lazy!

You're a cheater! Every time we play together you break the rules and I'm tired of it.

You're always late! I'm sick of wasting my time waiting around for you.

You never text me back! I guess we just won't be friends anymore.

You need to stop yelling! You are freaking out over nothing.

You always leave me out! You are a lousy friend.

- Marker board, chalkboard, or poster board with the following statement format written large enough for all to see:

I feel _____
         (name the feeling)

when _____
         (observation)

and I would like/would you be willing to _____
(say what you would like to happen instead).

INSTRUCTIONS

1. Explain that an "I-statement" is a format for sharing one's feelings about a situation without accusing the other person and resulting in their reacting defensively.

2. Review the statement format.

3. Explain that by beginning statements with "I feel" rather than "you are," our statements are less aggressive and accusatory. We are still conveying how we feel, but in a manner that is less likely to escalate a conflict.

4. Distribute the sentence strips and ask circle members to take a typical conflict comment and transform it into an "I-statement." One by one, circle members will read the original statement and then determine how to better phrase it using the "I-statement" format.

5. Once complete, discuss the following questions: Why do you think using I-statements deescalates conflicts? What might you find difficult about using I-statements?

Create a Family Talking Stick

As described in Part II, the Talking Stick is a tool traditionally used by Native Americans when a council is called. It is a visual cue of who has the right to talk during the gathering. The Talking Stick is passed from person to person as their turn comes to speak. Only one person is allowed to speak at a time. This method encourages other council members to listen to the speaker and to be respectful of the person's viewpoint during their turn with the Talking Stick. Using a Talking Stick promotes peaceful resolutions.

For this Integrated Activity, mothers and sons will create their own family Talking Stick to symbolize the skills of healthy communication and to remind circle participants to: be a good listener, consider and respect the other person's point of view, work together to think of solutions, and learn to relax the body and calm the mind in high-tension situations.

SUPPLIES

- An attractive wooden stick 6 to 15 inches in length – one per mother/son pair.
- Feathers
- Beads
- Other various nature items
- Colored ribbons
- Acrylic paint and brushes
- Sandpaper cut into 3-inch squares
- Soft cloth
- Craft glue

INSTRUCTIONS

1. Clean the stick with a soft cloth. Peel away any rough bark. Gently sand the stick until it is smooth and satin-like when touched.

2. Decorate the stick with the various decorations provided. Craft glue can be used to secure the items. Leave a smooth space on one end to act as a handle.

3. Mothers and sons together, think of a list of commitments as to how and when to use your new Talking Stick.

Quote Study

Peace cannot be kept by force; it can only be achieved by understanding.

Albert Einstein

....

If we have no peace, it is because we have forgotten that we belong to each other.

Mother Teresa

....

Peace is a journey of a thousand miles and it must be taken one step at a time.

Lyndon B. Johnson

....

Peace is not absence of conflict, it is the ability to handle conflict by peaceful means.

Ronald Reagan

....

While you are proclaiming peace with your lips, be careful to have it even more fully in your heart.

Saint Francis of Assisi

....

Peace does not mean just to stop wars, but also to stop oppression and injustice.

Tawakkol Karman

....

Violence is a tragic expression of unmet needs.

Marshall Rosenberg

Good wishes alone will not ensure peace.

Alfred Nobel

....

If you want to make peace with your enemy, you have to work with your enemy. Then he becomes your partner.

Nelson Mandela

....

Peace is not merely a distant goal that we seek, but a means by which we arrive at that goal.

Martin Luther King, Jr.

....

Out beyond ideas of wrongdoing and rightdoing there is a field. I'll meet you there.

Rumi

....

Respect for the rights of others means peace.

Benito Juárez

....

We look forward to the time when the Power of Love will replace the Love of Power. Then will our world know the blessings of peace.

William E. Gladstone

....

Words are windows or they're walls, they sentence us, or set us free.

Ruth Bebermeyer

Heartwork

MOTHERS AND SONS

1. Establish the habit of peaceful, authentic communication at home. This month, hold a Family Council Meeting and use your Talking Stick to practice positive communication. Each family member should have an opportunity to "check in" and express how they feel, share what is troubling or challenging them (if anything), and explain what kind of help they need from other family members.

SONS

1. Practice using "I-statements." Record your experiences in your Journey Journal. How did it feel to use "I-statements?" What was the outcome?

2. Research a real-life peacebuilder, either from history or someone you know. Place a picture of this hero on your altar.

"I LISTEN TO MY INTUITION"

> *There is a voice inside of you that whispers all day long, I feel that this is right for me, I know that this is wrong. No teacher, preacher, parent, friend or wise man can decide what's right for you – just listen to the voice that speaks inside.*
> **Shel Silverstein**

Dear Mothers,

Often referred to as a "gut feeling," "instinct," "inner voice," or "sixth sense," intuition is a deep, brilliant and protective force *within all of us*. Our intuition originates in our body's desire to keep us safe and thriving. It is the ability to understand something immediately, without the need for conscious reasoning. It is the knowing or sensing of something beyond time, space, and reason, beyond the active use of prior knowledge and beyond the five senses. Through our intuition, we tap into our subconscious minds, which is where we "archive" all sorts of information that we don't necessarily remember or know on a conscious level. The wisdom gleaned from our intuition helps keep us safer and supports us in making decisions that are in alignment with our highest good.

Intuition and Gender Stereotypes

How often do we as a culture refer to this critical human ability as "*women's* intuition," or "*mother's* intuition?" We talk about intuition as if it were some kind of mysterious, supernatural skill to which only the female half of the population has access. The typical generalization is that women use intuition while men use logic. But, as we learned in Month Three, gender stereotypes are *socially-constructed myths* and expectations that then become self-fulfilling prophecies.

The truth is, men and women are born with equal access to their intuition. We all start out as intuitive children. However, because gender stereotypes often shame boys out of their more tender feelings (pain, sadness, fear), their inner voice of intuition – which speaks primarily through feelings – becomes silenced over time. According to Dr. Judith Orloff, author of *Guide to Intuitive Healing: Five Steps to Physical, Emotional, and Sexual Wellness*:

> *Men can be powerfully intuitive – they have the same capabilities as women. But in our culture, we view intuition as something that's warm and fuzzy, or not masculine, so men have often lost their touch with those feelings.*

"Women," Orloff continues, "are encouraged to be receptive to their inner thoughts, so it appears that they have more intuition than men. The reality is, girls are praised for being sensitive while boys are urged to be more linear in their thinking rather than listening to a feeling."

For our sons, it is imperative that we reverse this process. Intuition is not just a "feel good" topic; it can mean the difference between life and death.

Intuition as a Main Source of Safety

Adolescence is a dangerous time. Some of the most life-threatening risks that people take – reckless or drunk driving, binge drinking, smoking, experimenting with drugs, and unprotected sex – are especially common during the teen years. Our sons are frequently faced with potentially damaging choices and yet they do not have the experience of adults to guide their decisions. A sharp sense of intuition and a strong relationship with their inner wise self can prove to be invaluable.

In his book, *Protecting the Gift: Keeping Children and Teenagers Safe (and Parents Sane)*, renowned safety expert Gavin de Becker asserts that supporting children's intuition is the most powerful tool parents have to keep their children safe from danger. He recommends that parents explicitly tell their children about intuition, and guide them to listen to and trust their internal warning signals while they are still only whispers. This recommendation is the seat of our intention for this month's circle. With this knowledge, de Becker explains, "our children will react to smoke and not wait for fire. They will care less about protocol and politeness, and be comfortable saying and doing what needs to be said and done."

Intuition and Anxiety

Unfortunately, anxiety disorders are on the rise among children and teens today, affecting 25% of all adolescents. It is likely that a member of your circle – perhaps even your own beloved son – deals with anxiety and will need guidance to learn to differentiate between the voice of their anxiety and the voice of their intuition. For those of us that deal with anxiety, learning to listen to our intuition can be extra tricky because intuition and anxiety are similar in nature and are often experienced in the same areas of the body. If your son struggles with anxiety, know that the support of a trained therapist or counselor can prove invaluable in helping him to untangle which warning signals to heed, and which may be false alarms, related to previous experiences in need of empathy and healing.

This month, we are giving our sons a gift that will serve them for the rest of their lives: we are giving them the knowledge that they have a wise source *within* – their intuition – that they can call upon at any time for answers and guidance. We may never know the full extent of the positive impact this will have on their lives.

We are in this together.

Love, *Melia*

Topic Introduction

Our Affirmation this month is: "*I Listen to My Intuition.*"

Did you know that we all have an inner voice, an inner source of wisdom that speaks in our hearts, guiding us and protecting us throughout our lives? This loving voice is called *intuition*.

Intuition refers to a sense, gut feeling, hunch, or instinct that something is so, even without concrete evidence or definitive knowledge. Intuition is that feeling you get that you can't always explain. For example, have you ever been introduced to someone for the first time, and picked up on some sort of negative energy? Perhaps their presence made you uncomfortable, but you didn't know why? That feeling, that inner knowing, is what we mean by *intuition*.

The concept of intuition may be new for you, or you may only have a vague understanding of what it means. We don't talk about intuition very much in our culture, especially with boys and men, and this is unfortunate because intuition is one of the greatest "super powers" humans have. We are *all* born with intuition, but we must learn to recognize and honor it.

Our intuition communicates with us in myriad ways, through physical responses and emotional feelings. For example, when making a decision, you might notice that as you consider your options, one choice in particular makes your heart feel more expansive than the other choices. Or perhaps you receive insight from dreams, waking and simply *knowing* what to do. Your intuition takes multiple forms, and over time, you will come to know your intuition's favorite way to get your attention. You will come to rely on it for information just as you would any of your five senses.

Your intuition's primary goal is to protect your highest good, and keep you safely moving in the right direction. The often quiet source of inner wisdom is always communicating with you. As the hero of your own life, it is your job to *listen* for your intuition, *trust* yourself, and *act* with courage. When heroes find themselves in difficult situations, rather than looking to everyone on the outside, they know to pause, check in with themselves, and ask, "What's the right thing to do here?" and, "What feels right to me?" Your intuition will lead you in the best direction.

At times, listening to your intuition may be challenging and may require a lot of courage. Listening to your intuition may require you to change plans, reverse direction, break with tradition, rock the boat, challenge authority, or even go against your friends. It takes courage to follow what's true for you and to not ignore your inner guidance, even if it contradicts the world of outside appearances and opinions. But as safety expert Gavin de Becker tells us, "intuition is always right in at least two important ways: It is always in response to something and it always has your best interest at heart."

In every hero's heart is an inner source of wisdom. Beloved sons, as you journey from boy to man, let your intuition be your guide.

Discussion Prompts

1. Have you ever heard or felt your intuition speaking to you? In what ways does your intuition communicate with you?

2. Has there been a time in your life when you listened to your intuition and you are really glad you did, or a time you didn't and wish you had?

3. We have many different voices inside of us. In what ways are you able to differentiate between the voice of your intuition, and the voice of unhelpful anxiety?

4. Do you believe men and women, girls and boys, all have equal access to their intuition? Why or why not?

5. One of the greatest things you can do to cultivate a relationship with your intuition is to honor your feelings. Feelings are like a loudspeaker for your intuition. They serve as clues as to what is right or wrong for you. What relationship do you see between your feelings and your intuition?

6. The importance of intuition in science has been recognized down through the ages. Even Albert Einstein once said, "the only real valuable thing is intuition." What relationship do you see between intuition and discoveries, achievements, and accomplishments? How might listening to one's intuition lead to greater success?

7. What does this month's Affirmation, "*I Listen to My Intuition*," mean to you? In the coming month, what opportunities might you have to put this Affirmation into practice? What are some challenges you might face in putting this Affirmation into practice?

Integrated Activities

An Inner Compass

A great metaphor for intuition is a compass. Intuition is like an *internal* compass that guides us and allows us to know which direction is True North for our greatest safety and fulfillment.

For this Integrated Activity, mothers are invited to gift their sons their very own compass to symbolize the *inner* compass of intuition. Heartwork for the month will include learning how to operate their new compass!

SUPPLIES

Each mother brings one compass to gift her own son. These can be pocket sized or keychain sized, family heirlooms or purchased inexpensively at your local outdoors store.

INSTRUCTIONS

1. Explain the symbolism of the compass and the purpose of the gift and hold space for gift giving and gratitude.

2. This month's Heartwork involves learning to navigate with your compass. For now, use the gifted compasses and work together as a circle to locate the four cardinal directions: North, South, East and West.

The Scents of Intuition

This playful Integrated Activity allows you to tap into your intuition, choose scents, and create your own essential oil spray!

SUPPLIES

- A variety of at least ten different essential oils, such as lavender, patchouli, lemon, peppermint, clove, sweet orange, cinnamon, lemongrass, clary sage, etc.

- 2-ounce glass bottle with fine mist sprayer – one for each circle member. These can be purchased online or at most craft stores.

- Witch Hazel, one bottle

- Tablespoon measures

- Small funnels

- Distilled water

- A small bowl of coffee beans

INSTRUCTIONS

Before circle begins:

1. Make a list of the essential oils your circle will be using.

2. Cover each of the labels on the essential oil bottles with a white, nontransparent sticker (name tag labels work well for this) so that the names of the scents cannot be seen and write a number on each label.

3. Write the corresponding number on your list. For example: lavender- 1, patchouli- 2, lemon- 3, and so on.

During circle:

4. Display the essential oils (with names covered and unknown by the group) and distribute the glass bottles to each circle member.

5. Using the small funnels, each circle member adds 6 tablespoons of water and 2 tablespoons of witch hazel to their bottle and shakes it.

6. Using your sense of smell – and your sense of intuition – choose the scent that is right for you. Allow circle members an opportunity to sample all of the different smells. Smelling the bowl of coffee beans in between scents will help clear the sense of smell.

7. Each circle member selects a scent. Remember the number you chose!

8. Place 10-15 drops of the scent you selected into your glass bottle. Shake.

9. Gather as a circle and reveal the names of the scents corresponding with each number. Allow time for participants to discuss which scent they chose and share why. It is always fun to see the similarities and differences in choices!

10. Each member now has their own bottle of essential oil spray, created with their intuition. Encourage circle members to use their spray as part of their morning or evening routines, spraying it on their body, bed, clothing, or even just in the room as a reminder of this month's Affirmation.

Quote Study

Rather than defining intuition as some unreasoned faulty quirk, it is defined as truly the soul-speaking. Intuition senses the direction to go in for most benefit, it is self-preserving, has a grasp of underlying motive and intention, it chooses what will cause the least amount of fragment to the psyche.

Clarissa Pinkola Estés

....

When I come to one of those places where I can't see which way to turn next, my best response has been: to quiet my anxiety and focus on the voice of the guide within myself. There is a source of divine wisdom in us that simply knows. A nudge, an awareness, a dream, an intuitive flash, a gradual dawning, a gut reaction – guidance comes from within, step by tiny step.

Sue Monk Kidd

....

The only real valuable thing is intuition.

Albert Einstein

....

It is through science that we prove, but through intuition that we discover.

Henri Poincaré

....

Intuition is always right in at least two important ways; It is always in response to something and it always has your best interest at heart.

Gavin de Becker

Quiet the mind and the soul will speak.

Ma Jaya Sati Bhagavati

....

The more you trust your intuition, the more empowered you become, the stronger you become, and the happier you become.

Gisele Bündchen

....

It is always with excitement that I wake up in the morning wondering what my intuition will toss up to me, like gifts from the sea. I work with it and rely on it. It's my partner.

Jonas Salk

....

Intuition is seeing with the soul.

Dean Koontz

....

Our bodies have five senses: touch, smell, taste, sight, hearing. But not to be overlooked are the senses of our souls: intuition, peace, foresight, trust, empathy. The differences between people lie in their use of these senses; most people don't know anything about the inner senses while a few people rely on them just as they rely on their physical senses, and in fact probably even more.

C. Joybell C.

....

Intuition is the highest form of intelligence, transcending all individual abilities and skills.

Sylvia Clare

If prayer is you talking to God, then intuition is God talking to you.

Dr. Wayne Dyer

....

Intuition is a very powerful thing. More powerful than intellect.

Steve Jobs

....

The primary wisdom is intuition.

Ralph Waldo Emerson

Heartwork

1. Meditate.

When seeking the wisdom and clarity of your intuition, silence is a helpful tool. Meditation is an effective, easy, enjoyable way to slow down and sharpen your awareness. By listening to your inner voice in silence and meditation, so much can be revealed. At some point in the coming month, create time alone with yourself and give this basic meditation exercise a try! If you enjoy it, consider carving out a little time in your life for a daily meditation practice. It can be as simple as this:

- Set a timer for 5 minutes.
- Sit or lie comfortably and gently close your eyes. You will notice your awareness expanding already!
- Begin to notice your breath, making no effort to control or change it.
- Focus your attention on your breath and on how the body moves with each inhalation and exhalation. Notice the movement of your body as you breathe. Observe your chest, shoulders, rib cage, and belly.
- If your mind wanders (and your mind will likely wander), gently return your focus back to your breath. Continue breathing and relaxing until the timer signals completion and then gently open your eyes.

2.   Learn how to navigate with your compass.

With all the technology available to us today, compass-based navigation has become anti-quated. But knowing how to use a compass is a cool life skill we should all learn! It's pretty simple, too. Ask a family member or mentor to teach you. If they don't know how, learn together! A quick internet search of "how to use a compass" will offer a plethora of tutorials and how-to videos available on the web.

"I CARE FOR
MY BODY, MIND, AND SPIRIT"

The most powerful relationship you will ever have is the relationship with yourself.
Steve Maraboli

Dear Mothers,

Part of growing up and developing a sense of personal responsibility for a healthy life entails identifying what we need, finding healthy ways to meet those needs, and knowing that it's okay to do so. Self-care – the deliberate care of our own mental, physical, and emotional health – is a vital piece of the ongoing process of being human. Thankfully, the term "self-care" crossed over into the mainstream in 2016, becoming somewhat of a buzzword for the timeless tradition of personal improvement commitments. However, self-care is more than just a trend; self-care is a pre-requisite for a full and healthy life.

But have you noticed that the care tips distributed online and in the media are overwhelmingly framed as something just for women? If psychologists and physicians agree that caring for one's physical, emotional, and spiritual needs is foundational for optimum success, health, and happiness, then why are men and boys so often shut out of this conversation? I am sure you will not be surprised to learn that the root cause of this exclusion lies, once again, in gender stereotypes.

Self-care and Gender Stereotypes

Traditional notions of masculinity exclude any interests or traits that could be considered girlish – things like caring for one's physical appearance, emotional awareness, and spiritual development. Men are expected to be strong, impenetrable, and pride-driven creatures who build their worth on how much they can bear or handle. Needing to take care of themselves or take down-time is perceived by many men as weak. The results of these damaging stereotypes are that, when compared relative to women, men as a group don't recognize physical symptoms of illness in themselves, wait longer to seek medical help, and demonstrate poor compliance with medications and other medical advice. This lack of adequate physical self-care is part of the reason why men have a shorter average life expectancy than women.

The time is overdue for society to recognize the imperative for male self-care, and we are starting with our sons. This next generation of men will know of their right and their responsibility to practice self-care, not from an outlook of "me first," but rather from a place of "me too."

This month in circle, we will challenge gender stereotypes and explore the importance of all people caring for their bodies, minds, and spirits. We will address the basics of physical self-care – which is of particular importance during the rapidly developing years of adolescence – including healthy nutrition, adequate exercise, sufficient sleep, etc. We will consider ways to relax, nurture one's own heart and emotional self, and seek enriching and inspiring experiences. And finally, we will use this month as a spring board to discuss two very important, and often interconnected, issues: body image and drug abuse.

Boys and Body Image

Despite public perception, body image issues and eating disorders are not an exclusively female problem – they just present in different ways and often go unreported or undiagnosed in males. Rather than wishing to be thinner, as girls and women often do, boys and men may obsess over shaping their bodies to traditional and unnatural ideals of masculine physique, which is to say, highly muscular and toned. Recent research shows that boys as young as eight years old struggle with body image, and the proportion of teen males dissatisfied with their bodies has tripled over the last twenty-five years, from 15% of the population to 45%. A recent study published in the journal *Pediatrics* reported 40% of boys in middle and high school exercise regularly – and 90% at least occasionally – with the specific goal of "bulking up." According to the same study, 38% of middle and high school boys use protein supplements and 6% admit to having experimented with steroids.

Although we do not hear about body image issues for boys as often as we do for girls, the ramifications of male body obsession – compulsive weightlifting, crash dieting, using anabolic steroids, smoking for appetite suppression, and taking dangerous supplements – are just as serious. *Every* body is uniquely and perfectly designed, and caring for one's physical self is about how one *feels* and their overall internal and external health, not about achieving some unrealistic ideal.

It is crucial that we support a healthy body image in our sons. Body image is closely linked to self-esteem and poor self-esteem can lead to many negative consequences, including substance abuse.

Boys and Substance Use

According to the National Institute on Drug Abuse, the key risk periods for drug abuse occur precisely during the major life transitions our sons are currently undergoing. These transitions include significant changes in physical development (i.e. puberty) or social situations (transitioning from elementary school to middle school or from middle school to high school). Early adolescence is the period that children are likely to encounter drug use for the first time. Any program seeking to support young people must therefore include drug, alcohol, and tobacco resistance education. This is especially true for our sons.

Since its inception in 1971, the annual National Survey on Drug Use and Health in the United States continues to show that males abuse drugs at higher rates than females, and generally receive more drug offers at younger ages. Furthermore, gender stereotypes and male socialization patterns play a major role in the high rates of male alcohol and other drug use. In a society that expects boys to eschew emotional expressiveness and closeness with other males, intoxication stands out as the only socially-sanctioned "excuse" for displays of emotions and affection. *The Hero's Heart*, in its effort to increase boys' emotional intelligence and nurture their friendships, actually serves as effective drug and alcohol abuse prevention.

This month, we will strengthen our sons' personal commitments against drug abuse by offering them honest education, clear expectations, and explicit support. Some parents fear that talking with their children about alcohol and drugs "puts ideas in their head." But we must understand, *our sons are talking about alcohol and other drugs with their peers*. Yes, they are. Of course, this is not a one-time conversation we need to have; we will address the topic of alcohol and other drugs often with our sons as they travel through the teen years. This month's Heartwork is designed to support our efforts.

Heroes and Self-Care

Because we use the term "hero" as the thematic basis for this program, it is important that we do not inadvertently confuse our sons as to what we mean. We do *not* mean unhealthy self-sacrifice or martyrdom. We do *not* mean focusing so intently on others' needs that their own needs are eclipsed. This month we will make it crystal clear to our sons that heroic living includes honoring the needs of one's own body, mind, and spirit. In doing so, heroes are better able to offer the world the full expression of who they are and the gifts they bring. The importance of this month's topic cannot be overstated; how our sons think about and care for themselves will impact everything they do and every decision they make.

We are in this together.

Love, *Melia*

Topic Introduction

Our Affirmation this month is: "*I Care for My Body, Mind, and Spirit.*"

This month we are going to learn about the importance of befriending ourselves, loving ourselves, and doing what we can to make sure our own needs are met. This practice is called "self-care" and it is the basis for our well-being.

We are each responsible for our own lives, and as heroes, we are called to honor that responsibility just as we would anything else that is precious. Because we are multi-dimensional beings, good self-care means caring for all aspects of what makes us human – our bodies, our minds, and our spirits.

We must give proper attention and respect to our physical bodies. Our miraculous bodies are with us from the moment we are born until the moment we die; they are the physical container for our souls. Our bodies are sacred instruments we use to express ourselves and to experience life. What could be more important than taking care of our bodies? From our hands to our bones, muscles and blood, our bodies are the first tool, the foundation of our connection with life. How we care for our bodies determines how well they serve our goals.

We must also stimulate our intelligence, practice curiosity, and engage in experiences that increase our self-esteem, confidence, and resilience. Caring for ourselves means learning to recognize when it is right to say "no" to others so that we can better say "yes" to ourselves. It means protecting our minds from negative thoughts and behavior patterns.

And finally, we must take time for the things that bring us pleasure, relax us, and help us express our feelings and connect with others in positive ways.

It is important to understand that attending to our emotional, physical, and spiritual needs is a *daily* practice, not just a sporadic reward or special treat. A helpful metaphor is the concept of a bank account. With a bank account, we deposit and invest money *in*, so that later when needed, we can withdraw and take money *out*. In the same way, practicing self-care is like making nourishing 'deposits' into the bank account of your Self. When we have energetic 'funds' available through sufficient self-care, we are then able to make energetic 'withdrawals' to support our lives and relationships. Our goal is to always have sufficient funds and not deplete our energies and become bankrupt. The way for us to meet this goal is to care for ourselves – body, mind, and spirit – each day. Understandably, the maintenance of a self-care routine can be challenging during hard times or periods of high stress, but this is precisely when we need to invest in our own well-being the most.

Beloved sons, we want you to love yourselves and to know of your unique worth. You matter. Your life, your needs, your desires, and your dreams *matter*. The most powerful relationship you will ever have is the one you have with yourself, and our wish for you is that it is a relationship of kindness, gentleness, honor, and respect.

Heroes love and care for themselves. They keep their bodies, minds, and spirits nurtured and nourished, not just for themselves, but for the world.

Discussion Prompts

1. How do gender stereotypes impact the self-care practices of boys and men? Do you believe men need and deserve self-care? Does practicing self-care equate to weakness? Why or why not?

2. If you asked your body, mind, and spirit about how you practice self-care, what would they tell you?

3. How you feel about your body impacts how you treat it. Who or what supports you in developing a positive body image and accepting your body as it is? Who or what encourages you to treat your body with love and respect?

4. Most people understand that drugs, alcohol, and tobacco have destructive effects on the functions of the body, mind, and spirit. Why do people still choose to use them, even though they know about the damaging consequences? What influences a person's decision whether or not to use alcohol, tobacco, or other drugs?

5. Who are your self-care role models? What are the habits that you admire?

6. What does this month's Affirmation, "*I Care for My Body, Mind, and Spirit*," mean to you? In the coming month, what opportunity might you have to put this Affirmation into practice? What are some challenges you might face in practicing this month's Affirmation?

Integrated Activities

What's on Your Plate?

Each life is unique and has its own demands. When it comes to self-care, there is no 'one-size-fits-all' approach; we each must determine what self-care means for us and how to apply it in our lives. This integrated activity allows participants the opportunity to examine their lives and explores ideas to begin to design a personalized self-care plan specific to their needs.

SUPPLIES

- Paper plates. Enough for each circle member to have one.
- Colored markers, pens, colored pencils, etc.
- Circle stencils (cups or small bowls work well)

1. Discuss the analogy of "having a full plate" as it represents someone's responsibilities and commitments. Ask circle members to think about what is "on their plate," i.e. what they have to get done each day – their responsibilities, work or school tasks, hobbies, stressors, etc.

2. Distribute the paper plates and markers. Ask participants to decorate the front of the paper plate with symbols, drawings, or words that represent the obligations, tasks, and interests that are "on their plate."

3. Hold space for circle members to share some of the items on their plate. The group will likely hear many commonalities, and at the same time, will learn about some of the unique stressors, responsibilities, or interests of other circle members.

4. Instruct circle members to turn their plates over and, on the back side of the paper plate, use the circle stencils to draw three interlocking circles representing Body, Mind, and Spirit. You may wish to use different colors for each circle. Label the circles with the area of self-care they represent.

5. Explain to the circle that we all have "full plates." To accomplish our goals and meet our responsibilities, we must take good care of ourselves – body, mind, and spirit. Comment on how the three realms are interconnected and impact one another and our overall well-being.

6. Invite circle members to brainstorm different ways they will practice self-care in each of the domains. For example, exercise, get enough sleep, make healthy food choices, drink water, share feelings with a trusted friend or family member, take a warm bath, get a massage, take a break from screens, read an inspiring book, meditate, play outside, go for a walk in nature, keep doctor and dental appointments, take prescription medications as instructed, avoid drugs and alcohol, make a phone call to a Hero's Heart brother, attend faith services, listen to a favorite song, journal, see a counselor, cuddle with an animal, learn a new skill, etc.

7. Invite circle members to share some of their ideas and inspire one another.

Meditation: The Skin I'm In

The human body is a miracle! When we excessively place our value and focus on how our bodies look on the outside, we often forget all of the incredible things our bodies do for us, day in and day out, on the inside. Appreciating our bodies for all the complex internal biological functions they perform is a great way to re-shape the dialogue we have with ourselves about our bodies and create a more positive body image.

INSTRUCTIONS

Read the following meditation aloud to your circle, and together, take a journey inward to observe the amazing instrument of the body.

Take a deep breath in and as you exhale, imagine that your consciousness is so light that it can float up and out of your physical body. In your mind's eye, allow yourself to gently rise up above your body, and see yourself, just as you are, here in our circle.

With loving compassion and unconditional acceptance, observe your physical body from this vantage point. Take a moment now to see yourself as you would gaze upon a beloved friend. Feel in your heart the unconditional love and gratitude for all that your body does for you.

Notice the largest organ of your body — your skin. Your skin defines the limit between yourself and the rest of the universe. It protects and contains you. Take a moment now to tune in to your skin. Ask your skin what it wants and needs, and listen to its reply. Thank your skin for its devotion to you.

I invite you now to shift your consciousness to your muscles and bones and joints — the parts that move you. Your body was built to move! Tune in with your bones and muscles now, and ask your musculoskeletal system what it wants and needs. What movement does your body crave? What physical practice would nourish and strengthen you? Thank your muscles and bones for their devotion to you.

And now shift your awareness to your cardiovascular and respiratory systems — your heart, lungs, and blood. The home of your breath and seat of your emotional body, your lungs and heart work without rest to fuel your body with oxygen and nourishment for all of the work and play and passion that you choose. Ready in an instant, your cardiovascular and respiratory systems are on stand-by 24/7 to serve you. I invite you now to tune in with your heart, and lungs, and blood and ask them what they want and need. Feel the rhythm and the pulse of your body, and thank your heart and blood and lungs for their devotion to you.

I invite you now to shift your awareness to your digestive system — your stomach and intestines. Tasked with sorting through all that you eat and drink, and separating the nourishing from the unusable, your digestive system keeps your cells fueled and functional. Take a moment now to tune in with your digestive system. Gently, kindly, ask your digestive system what would nurture and nourish it, and listen for the answer. Thank your digestive system for its devotion to you.

And lastly, I invite you to shift your awareness to your nervous system – your brain and nerves. The control center of your physical body, your nervous system makes the commands and fires them out while seamlessly integrating the incoming data stream from all of your five senses and also thinking thoughts and dreaming dreams and analyzing information without you being consciously aware of it all happening! That is quite a feat! Breathing in now a sense of well-being and calm, I invite you to tune in with your nervous system and ask it what it most needs and wants; what would offer calming nourishment? Listen for the answer. Thank your nervous system for its devotion to you.

With a deep breath in, I invite you now to gently rejoin your physical self, reintegrate your consciousness and your body. Feel the weight of your trunk and legs being supported by your seat. Feel the rhythm of your heart, and the cycling of your breath. When you are ready, open your eyes.

Following the meditation, hold space for sharing and reflection among circle participants.

- *What was your experience with this meditation?*
- *What wants and needs did your various body systems communicate?*
- *How did it feel to offer gratitude to your body?*
- *How might you incorporate this kind of conversation with your body on a daily basis?*

Drug and Alcohol Resistance Role-Play

We should expect that at some point in the adolescent years, someone is going to offer our sons a cigarette, e-cigarette, smokeless tobacco, alcoholic drink, illicit drug, or other intoxicating substance. Many youths are caught off-guard and acquiesce simply because they were not prepared for handling such a scenario. This Integrated Activity allows participants an opportunity to consider ways to decline alcohol and other drugs in different social situations. However, the point is not simply to prepare for these particular scenarios, but to stimulate open and honest conversation among mothers and sons.

Divide circle members into groups of two or three participants and assign each group one of the scenarios below. Encourage participants to assign character roles and practice their role-play together before performing it for the circle.

Scenario One

You are at a classmate's house working together on a project. His parents are not home. He takes a bottle of spray paint and begins to sniff it. He says you should sniff the paint too because it will give you "a nice high and make the work go by more quickly." You really like this person and don't want to embarrass yourself, but you also don't want to inhale chemicals.

Scenario Two

Your parents have dropped you and a friend off at the movie theater. As you are walking in, your friend takes out a vape pen and candy-flavored e-liquid from his pocket and says, "Hey, let's skip the movie and go try this out." You like this friend, but you don't want to vape.

Scenario Three

You are working at a summer job mowing lawns. When you are finished for the day, one of your coworkers offers you a beer to "relax and cool off with the guys." You are the youngest employee and you want to feel like part of the group, but you also don't want to drink the beer.

Scenario Four

You are riding on the school bus, on the way to a football game. One of your teammates opens his bag and reveals a twelve-pack of small, highly caffeinated energy drinks. He wants you each to drink six to "play faster and stronger." You really want to do well at the game, but you don't want to drink so many of the dangerous drinks.

Scenario Five

You are home alone watching television, feeling rather bored. A neighbor a few years older than you stops by to deliver some mail that was accidentally delivered to his house. He asks you how you are doing and when you mention how bored you are, he shows you a marijuana joint in his pocket and invites you over to his house to get high. You don't want to smoke pot.

Scenario Six

You are at a party with some of the most popular kids in school. You are having a great time and finally feel like part of the "in" crowd. Halfway through the party, the party host, a girl you really like, pours liquor from her parents' cabinet into everyone's soda. Everyone is laughing about it and talking about "getting wasted." You don't want to drink alcohol.

Quote Study

When you recover or discover something that nourishes your soul and brings joy, care enough about yourself to make room for it in your life.

Jean Shinoda Bolen

....

We have to accept personal responsibility for uplifting our lives.

Chögyam Trungpa

....

Nurture your minds with great thoughts. To believe in the heroic makes heroes.

Benjamin Disraeli

....

If your compassion does not include yourself, it is incomplete.

Jack Kornfield

....

When you say 'yes' to others, make sure you are not saying 'no' to yourself.

Paulo Coehlo

....

You are the sum total of everything you've ever seen, heard, eaten, smelled, been told, forgot — it's all there. Everything influences each of us, and because of that, I try to make sure that my experiences are positive.

Maya Angelou

There are days I drop words of comfort on myself like falling leaves and remember that it is enough to be taken care of by myself.

Brian Andreas

....

Growing into your future requires a dedication to caring for yourself as if you were rare and precious, which you are, and all life around you as equally so, which it is.

Victoria Moran

....

Self-care is never a selfish act – it is simply good stewardship of the only gift I have, the gift I was put on earth to offer others.

Parker Palmer

....

You yourself, as much as anybody in the entire universe, deserve your love and affection.

Buddha

....

Enjoy your body, use it every way you can. Don't be afraid of it, or what other people think of it, it's the greatest instrument you'll ever own.

Kurt Vonnegut

....

Self-care is not selfish or self-indulgent. We cannot nurture others from a dry well. We need to take care of our own needs first, then we can give from our surplus, our abundance.

Jennifer Louden

Don't let your mind bully your body.

June Tomaso Wood

....

I'm serious about no alcohol, no drugs. Life is too beautiful.

Jim Carrey

Heartwork

MOTHERS

1. At some point every day this month, check in with your son about his needs. Prompt him by asking, "What do you think your mind/body/spirit needs right now?" and "What are some ways you could meet those needs?"

2. Continue the conversation on drug and alcohol resistance together at home. Ask your son what curiosities or questions he has about drugs and alcohol. Share your views, family rules, and expectations with him.

3. Exercise can quickly transform negative energy into positive energy, and even a gentle walk outside is enough to release "feel good" endorphins and relieve stress. Our bodies are not meant to be inactive, but in today's world, the opportunities for physical activity often need to be created. This month, make it a point to go for a walk outside together and notice how great it makes you both feel!

SONS

1. At the beginning of each week, draw the three interlocking circles from this month's Integrated Activity in your Journey Journal. At the end of each day, reflect on the care you gave yourself in each domain – body, mind, and spirit. For each act of self-care, regardless of how small or large, place a single tally mark in the corresponding realm. At the end of the week, notice the distribution of tally marks. Are you more caring in some areas than others? Consider ways to create even more balance and care in the coming week. Draw a new set of circles in your Journey Journal and start again.

2. The media and advertising industry often glamorize alcohol, tobacco, and drug usage. The messages tend make it look like a person will have more fun and be more popular if they get drunk or high, while glossing over any negative consequences. This month, notice the messages you receive from the web, commercials, movies, and television shows about drug and alcohol use. How do these messages make you feel? What information do they include and what do they leave out? Practice critical thinking skills to decode the real message they are trying to send.

3. If you are on social media, take an inventory of all the pages and people you follow, asking yourself: How does viewing this page/person make me feel about myself? Is this page/person a positive or negative addition to my life? How might this page/person be influencing how I care for myself? Listen to your intuition and unfollow/unfriend/unlike any person or page that does not serve your highest good.

"I HONOR MY CHANGING BODY"

> " *I stand in awe of my body.*"
>
> **Henry David Thoreau**

Dear Mothers,

Change is on the horizon. It seems like just yesterday we were reading *Goodnight Moon* to our little boys, and now – right before our eyes – they are beginning the gradual process of growing into young men. Recent demographic studies indicate puberty in boys is starting earlier than ever before, as early as nine years old. From the ages of nine to fifteen, boys begin to experience a major growth spurt; erections and sexual urges become nascent, pubic, underarm and facial hair grows, perspiration increases, muscles develop, the penis, testes, and scrotum enlarge, breasts can temporarily swell, the voice "breaks" and becomes permanently deeper, acne may develop, and ejaculation and nocturnal emissions begin to occur. In addition to these dramatic physical changes, puberty also brings about profound emotional and social changes. Mother Nature insists that our sons undergo a tremendous amount of change in a relatively short amount of time!

As our sons develop, they are certain to have questions and concerns about the changes of puberty. Some of our sons will naturally be more expressive and open during puberty, freely coming to us to share their experiences, while others will be more reserved and wonder about these things privately or perhaps rely on misinformation from peers. We should answer questions as they come, but perhaps more importantly, we must not wait for our sons to come to us. Just as we proactively prepare our children for what to expect with other life changes, such as starting school, welcoming a new member into the family, or taking a city bus alone for the first time, our sons need to know what to expect with puberty – before it starts.

Misinformation abounds among peer groups as young adolescents grapple with the new things they are experiencing. Many concerns that kids have throughout puberty arise simply because the kids don't know that the changes and issues they are facing are normal. Given that puberty can begin as early as age nine for boys and eight for girls, Dr. Fred Kaesar, author of *What Your Child Needs to Know About Sex (and When)*, recommends that by age eight, both boys and girls know the bodily changes that are associated with puberty. This month's circle curriculum is designed to guide you step-by-step through one of the many important conversations you will have with your son about puberty over the next five or so years. We will address the physical, emotional, and social changes of puberty, in addition to two of the more serious issues our growing boys will encounter: pornography and sexual harassment.

The Elephant on the Screen

When we were teenagers, serious pornography was mostly inaccessible. The modern Internet and mobile technology have completely changed the landscape of opportunities for exposure to pornography. Our kids are not just seeing still, nude photographs in Playboy magazines. More often than not, the search results they encounter are violently misogynistic, devoid of intimacy, and completely unrealistic.

Regardless of your personal opinions on pornography, we can all agree it is not for children. In fact, it is illegal for people under age eighteen to view pornography. And yet, these are the facts:

- Your child will most likely be exposed to pornography. Ninety percent of boys and 60% of girls view pornography before their eighteenth birthday. Statistically, the average first exposure children have to online pornography is age eleven. It is very likely that your son is going to either come across pornography, seek it out, or a friend will show it to him (if this hasn't already happened).

- Pornography is unavoidable. With the proliferation of smartphones and other wireless devices with internet connections, there exists an unprecedented opportunity for anyone to view hardcore pornography with just one free click. We can (and should) screen and monitor our sons' media exposure, but as they get older this becomes more challenging.

- Viewing pornography can lead to addiction, and can negatively influence children's sexual development, relationships, and attitudes. The long-term effects of adolescent pornography viewing are not yet known.

We must talk directly with our sons about pornography. We must address the proverbial "elephant on the screen." This month in circle, we are going to explain to our sons what pornography is exactly and why it can be harmful to their growing brains. This month's Heart-work assignment encourages you to speak further with your son about your family's rules and expectations regarding pornography. To be clear: it is not the details of sex or sex education from which we are protecting our sons (in fact, next month is dedicated to this very topic!), but rather the harmful miseducation found in the vast majority of pornography.

Boys Will Be Respectful Men

2017 was a momentous year for survivors of sexual harassment and assault. Following the disturbing Harvey Weinstein scandal, women all over the world came forward and shared their own stories of sexual harassment and abuse with the explosive 'Me Too' movement on social media. As woman after brave woman contributed to the #metoo compendium, many sharing the details of their heartbreaking stories, we could no longer deny the pervasiveness of the problem. These courageous "Silence Breakers" were named Time Magazine's 2017 Person of the Year, and our collective eyes were opened to the prevalence of sexual violence against girls and women; we worried for our daughters, and the wisest among us looked to our sons and how we are raising them.

Sexual harassment and assault do not happen in a vacuum and the perpetrators cannot be conveniently written off as evil monsters. The ubiquitous sexual violence against women is a result of living in a patriarchal culture that normalizes misogynistic language, objectifies women's bodies, and glamorizes sexual violence. We cannot just hope our sons will not be affected by this culture and will not become "those" men; we must take action to ensure it.

Earlier this year, researchers from Harvard University released a ground-breaking report summarizing the results of a national survey of eighteen to twenty-five year olds. Of the respondents, 87% reported having experienced at least one of the following during their lifetime: being catcalled (55%), touched without permission by a stranger (41%), insulted with sexualized words by a man (47%), having a stranger say something sexual to them (52%), and having a stranger tell them they were "hot" (61%). Yet, 76% of the male and female respondents had *never had a conversation with their parents about how to avoid sexually harassing others.* This lack of parental education is not acceptable. If we are to change the culture of sexual victimization, we must have direct discussions with not only our daughters regarding their safety, but also our sons regarding their responsibility.

Next month, we will cover the topic of consent, and this month, we will hold space for a frank discussion on the importance of respecting women – all women – and honoring their bodies.

You Can Do It!

If you feel nervous talking to your son about these issues, you are not alone. Most parents feel uncomfortable or embarrassed talking with their sons about certain topics, like their bodies. For mothers, this topic can feel especially daunting since we have not experienced some of the particular physical changes firsthand. However, our job is still to guide our sons through uncharted territory, just as we always have.

I encourage you to follow your circle's lead this month. Above all, keep the following key messages at the forefront of your heart so that your son will hear, in between the lines of the circle discussion, that:

1. **Your body is holy.** The changes that are happening to your body are good, natural, and healthy. We celebrate and honor your unique process of puberty.

2. **Women's and girls' bodies are holy.** We expect you to treat women and girls with respect and honor.

3. **We are here for you.** There is nothing we cannot talk about and there is nothing you could say or ask that would shock us, scare us, or make us think less of you.

Teaching your son about his body should be an open, honest, and ongoing conversation. The more comfortable we are, the more effective our communication will be. If a question or comment stumps you in circle, or in your private conversations with your son, it is perfectly fine to say, "That is a great question and I'm so glad you asked me. I don't know the answer yet. Let's research it together." Or "Let me think about that and get back to you." Just make sure you follow through with an answer.

You can do this, mamas!

We are in this together.

Love, *Melia*

Topic Introduction

Our Affirmation this month is: "*I Honor My Changing Body.*"

Beloved sons, you are at the age of a special phase of your life called puberty. Puberty is the time when a person's body, feelings, and relationships transition from a child's towards an adult's. It is the process of turning from a boy into a man, or from a girl into a woman, and it lasts several years.

Everyone goes through puberty, and the changes of puberty occur at different times in their life. For example, some girls start noticing the changes of puberty as young as eight or nine years old, while other girls may not start puberty until age twelve or thirteen. Some boys start noticing the chances of puberty as young as nine or ten years old, or maybe not until thirteen or fourteen. One of the most important things for you to understand when it comes to puberty is: variation is normal. The timing, speed, and order that your body goes through the changes of puberty is right for you.

We believe that knowledge is power, and so we want you to be knowledgeable about the changes that are soon happening to your body. You have the right to know what to expect. This month in circle, we are going to discuss the physical, emotional, and social changes that come with puberty.

Many people at your age feel uncomfortable talking about the changes they are experiencing or will soon experience. You might feel excited, embarrassed, stressed, or worried. Rest assured that, as always, there is no pressure to speak or share in circle. You may wish to simply listen and write your thoughts and questions in your Journey Journal. That is perfectly okay! At the same time, you will have ample opportunity to ask questions and share your thoughts if you wish. It's normal to think about the changes happening in your body and to want to know more. The best way to overcome any feelings of embarrassment is to learn about what is happening.

To honor something means to treat it with great admiration and respect. During this important phase of your life, we wish for you to honor your changing body, and we expect you to honor girls' and women's bodies as well.

With honor, we celebrate who you are and we look joyfully to who you are becoming!

Discussion Prompts

1. What is one thing you are anxious about and one thing you are excited about when it comes to puberty and growing up?

2. People often use slang words for reproductive body parts and body processes. Using these words can make it easier to objectify body parts, and can make the body seem "taboo" or like something we aren't really supposed to talk about. Out of reverence and respect for our bodies, it is important to know and use the real vocabulary. What slang words have you heard? Why do you think people use slang words for body parts? Why is it important to use the real words?

3. Because puberty starts at different times for everyone, some kids will develop secondary sexual characteristics earlier than their peers and some later. Many times, these earlier or later developing kids can become targets for bullying and harassment, which is never okay. Has this ever happened to you or someone you know? How did you handle it?

4. Pornography is pictures, videos, or even cartoons of people with few or no clothes on, often depicting sexual activities. However, pornographic sex is not *real* sex; pornography doesn't usually show the loving, emotional aspects of sex, and often portrays women as objects. Many kids see pornography by accident on computers, phones, or other devices. Sometimes kids are shown pornography by a friend or even a family member. This should

never happen because pornography is not for kids. The concern is not so much with you seeing sex, but with the way sex is presented. The media tends to depict sex as the man as being dominant and the woman being passive, or even being treated with aggression and violence or as an act of anger. In pornography, sex is shown as something that men do **to** women and not **with** them. That is not what real sex is and that is not how we want you to think of sex. As they get older, boys and girls alike become curious about what sex is and how it is done. Interest in sex is healthy, but what you find online probably won't be. If you have seen pornography, you have probably had a reaction of knowing immediately that it felt wrong. You may have felt embarrassed or sick to your stomach. At the same time, it may have felt exciting or interesting to you and you wanted to keep looking at it. Viewing pornography can hurt your growing heart and mind, and damage your future relationships because it lies to your brain about how people should treat one another. Viewing pornography can even lead to a consuming habit or addiction, because once you see it, your brain wants to see more and more of it. How do you feel about pornography? Have you ever thought about how pornography portrays women, men, and sex? How will you protect your growing heart and mind from pornography?

5. Heroes respect girls and women, and they know that it is never acceptable to talk in a disrespectful way about *anyone's* body. Have you ever heard someone comment in an objectifying way about a girl's body, or tell a distasteful joke about women and sexual behavior? Why do you think this happens? How might someone feel after experiencing verbal sexual harassment? As a hero, how will you challenge this kind of dishonoring sexual language or harassment when you encounter it? What will you say and do?

6. Masturbation is when a boy or girl touches, rubs, or strokes their genitals in a way that makes them feel good. Masturbation is a private experience that should be done in a private place, like your bedroom. It is normal, healthy, and safe. Throughout history, however, some cultures and religions have opposed masturbation and even labeled it as sinful. This is unfortunate because privately exploring your own body should never make anyone feel guilty or shameful. What cultural messages have you received about masturbation?

7. What does this month's Affirmation, "*I Honor My Changing Body*," mean to you? In the coming month, what opportunity might you have to put this Affirmation into practice? What are some challenges you might face in practicing this month's Affirmation?

Integrated Activities

Boy/Girl/Both

Boys and girls have some similar and some different experiences during puberty. In this Integrated Activity, your circle will explore the key physical, emotional, and social changes of puberty in an open and reverent way, while encouraging dialogue and questions.

SUPPLIES

- 30 Index Cards
- Pen
- 3 empty gift bags

INSTRUCTIONS

1. Before circle begins, write the following words on the front and back of the index cards:

....

Card 1

[FRONT] GROW TALLER

[BACK] Both. One of the first things people notice about puberty is a fast growth spurt. Because everyone starts puberty at different times, you could find yourself growing much faster or slower than your peers.

....

Card 2

[FRONT] SKIN GETS OILY

[BACK] Both. During puberty, oil glands on the face become more active in both boys and girls.

....

Card 3

[FRONT] ACNE (PIMPLES)

[BACK] Both. Almost everyone gets pimples on their face when they are going through puberty. People can also get them on their backs, or other parts of their body.

....

Card 4

[FRONT] VOICE CHANGES

[BACK] Both. Boys and girls both experience changes in their vocal quality, pitch, and resonance during puberty, but the changes are much more pronounced for boys. During puberty, your voice begins the process of changing into a man's voice. During this process, your voice will probably become a little croaky – sometimes a low rumble, and sometimes squeaky, even in the same sentence.

Card 5

[FRONT] HAIR GROWS ON FACE

[BACK] Both. Some girls get thicker or darker hair on their upper lip during puberty. For boys, facial hair first appears at the corners of your lips, and then spreads across your upper lip, to the upper part of your cheek, below the bottom lip, and finally to the sides of your face and chin. Some boys shave their facial hair and others do not. It is your choice.

Card 6

[FRONT] HAIR GETS OILY

[BACK] Both. During puberty, both boys' and girls' oil glands become more active, and this may mean their hair gets oilier.

Card 7

[FRONT] HAIR GROWS IN ARMPITS

[BACK] Both. During puberty, hair starts to grow under the arms. Some girls choose to shave their underarm hair, and others do not. It is their choice.

Card 8

[FRONT] HAIR GROWS ON AND AROUND GENITALS (PUBIC HAIR)

[BACK] Both. The first place you will see hair growing is around your penis and testicles. To start with, it's quite thin and only grows in a small patch. After about a year, it gets thicker, curlier, and spreads outward. Girls grow pubic hair – on and above their vulva – as well. The purpose of pubic hair is to keep that area of the body clean and to keep the skin from chaffing.

Card 9

[FRONT] SWEAT GLANDS DEVELOP

[BACK] Both. As people grow up, they start to sweat more, which is normal and healthy. When sweat mixes with natural bacteria on the skin and meets the air, people can experience body odor.

Card 10

[FRONT] BREASTS DEVELOP

[BACK] Both. During puberty, most boys experience some soreness and tenderness around their nipples, and nearly half of all boys will have some slight swelling in the breast area under the nipples. This is just fatty tissue and it will disappear as boys grow. Girls develop breasts during puberty in preparation for milk production if they decide to have a baby one day.

Card 11

[FRONT] HIPS GET WIDER

[BACK] Girls. During puberty, girls' hips and thighs grow wider.

Card 12

[FRONT] SHOULDERS GET WIDER

[BACK] Boys. During puberty, boys' shoulders grow wider.

Card 13

[FRONT] START PRODUCING SPERM

[BACK] Boys. Sperm are tiny, tadpole-shaped cells that men produce in their testicles. Sperm comes out of a man's penis in semen when he ejaculates. Sperm can fertilize a woman's egg to make her pregnant.

Card 14

[FRONT] TESTICLES GET BIGGER

[BACK] Boys. In puberty, hormones cause the testicles to grow bigger. The skin of the scrotum (the sac that hangs beneath the penis and contains the testicles) becomes thinner and hangs lower. One testicle often hangs lower than the other.

Card 15

[FRONT] PENIS GROWS BIGGER

[BACK] Boys. Boys' penises grow longer and wider during puberty. Penises come in all different sizes. All sizes are good and big enough for the job they were intended to do. When the body gets cold or anxious, the penis and scrotum shrivel up somewhat. This is normal and temporary.

Card 16

[FRONT] NOCTURNAL EMISSIONS (WET DREAMS)

[BACK] Boys. Some boys wake up to find that they have ejaculated semen in their sleep. Semen is wet, and leaves a mark on your pajamas or sheets, but it washes out easily. Some boys have a lot of wet dreams and some boys rarely or never do. Both are totally normal and healthy. There is no reason to feel guilty or embarrassed when you experience a wet dream. It is an involuntary (which means uncontrollable), normal, and healthy part of puberty.

Card 17

[FRONT] ERECTIONS HAPPEN MORE FREQUENTLY

[BACK] Boys. Erections are when your penis fills with blood, causing it to get hard and point up and away from your body. As boys go through puberty, they get erections often – probably every day. If this happens to you in front of people, it is best to relax, focus on something else, and try not to worry about it. Erections go away after a few minutes, and other people are never as focused on us as we imagine them to be.

Card 18

[FRONT] EXPERIENCE EJACULATION

[BACK] Boys. Ejaculation is when sperm shoots out of the end of your penis from stimulation or during nocturnal emissions. Ejaculation does not happen in males until they begin producing sperm during puberty.

Card 19

[FRONT] MUSCLES BECOME MORE DEVELOPED

[BACK] Boys. Toward the end of puberty, boys begin to develop muscle mass and strength, particularly upper body strength. Girls do too, but usually less so.

Card 20

[FRONT] GAIN WEIGHT

[BACK] Both. Both boys and girls gain weight during puberty.

Card 21

[FRONT] MOOD SWINGS

[BACK] Both. Mood swings – alternating quickly between energetic and happy, then glum and moody – are a side-effect of the hormones in your body. Both boys and girls experience mood swings during puberty.

Card 22

[FRONT] START HAVING SEXUAL THOUGHTS AND FEELINGS

[BACK] Both. Both boys and girls can start feeling sexually attracted to other people in puberty, and may imagine touching or kissing them. Fantasizing in this way is safe and natural.

Card 23

[FRONT] SOMETIMES FEEL LONELY AND CONFUSED

[BACK] Both. Boys and girls can sometimes feel a bit "down" as a result of all the hormonal changes of puberty. It is important to be extra gentle with yourself, practice self-care, and know that the heavy feelings will pass.

Card 24

[FRONT] LEG HAIR THICKENS AND MAY BECOME DARKER OR COARSER.

[BACK] Both. During puberty, both boys' and girls' leg hair thickens and may become darker or coarser. Some girls choose to shave their leg hair and some girls don't. It is their choice.

Card 25

[FRONT] SOMETIMES FEEL EMBARRASSED OR SELF-CONSCIOUS ABOUT THEIR CHANGING BODY

[BACK] Both. Both boys and girls often experience feelings of insecurity about their appearance as they go through puberty.

Card 26

[FRONT] START RELEASING EGGS (OVULATION)

[BACK] Girls. Approximately once a month, one egg from one ovary is released into the nearest fallopian tube. The egg is present for about twenty-four hours after ovulation. During this time, if the egg joins with a sperm cell (which can survive for days in a woman's body), it can then attach itself to the lining in the uterus and grow into a baby.

Card 27

[FRONT] START MENSTRUATING (PERIODS)

[BACK] Girls. If a woman's egg isn't fertilized by sperm, it's shed along with the soft lining in her uterus (which is mostly made up of blood) through her vagina. This bleeding lasts for a few days, and happens approximately once a month.

Card 28

[FRONT] START PRODUCING VAGINAL DISCHARGE

[BACK] Girls. During puberty, girls begin to produce a small amount of clear, whitish liquid from their vaginas. This discharge is normal and helps to keep the vagina healthy.

Card 29

[FRONT] FEEL AWKWARD AT TIMES AROUND THE PEOPLE TO WHICH YOU FEEL ATTRACTION

[BACK] Both. During puberty, it is normal for both boys and girls to feel excited, nervous, or awkward around the people they feel attracted to at times.

Card 30

[FRONT] MAY GET AN 'ADAM'S APPLE'

[BACK] Boys. During puberty, your larynx (voice box) gets larger and may become visible as a lump in the front of your throat.

2. Label the three gift bags – **Boys**, **Girls**, **Both**. Place the empty gift bags on the altar. Explain to the circle that these bags represent the 'gifts' of puberty that happen – some only to boys, some only to girls, and some to both boys and girls.

3. Distribute the index cards among circle members.

4. Going around the circle, give each member an opportunity to read the front of their card aloud to the group. Invite guesses as to whether the listed change happens to boys, girls, or both boys and girls. After the guesses have been made, the circle member will read the back of the card and place it in the corresponding bag. Encourage questions and discussion after each card before moving on to the next circle member's turn. Remind the circle that if someone has a question or comment they would rather not share with the entire circle, they can write a note in their Journey Journal to discuss with their mother at a later time.

Two Truths and a Lie

Puberty and growing up is an exciting time that can also be confusing. You will get lots of information – some true and some false – from your peers and the media. It is important to sort out what is true and what is not. This Integrated Activity offers an educational twist on a fun, classic group game.

SUPPLIES

- A selection of age-appropriate books (see the Recommended Resources at the back of this book for title suggestions) on male and female sexual anatomy, physiology, and puberty development – enough for each mother/son pair to have one book.
- Pens
- Blank paper for note-taking

INSTRUCTIONS

1. Split into mother/son pairs.

2. Using the provided books as your guide, each pair writes down two facts (truths) about male or female anatomy, physiology, and/or puberty development, and one myth (lie). For example:

- *Females are born with all the eggs they will ever have. (Truth)*
- *Males begin producing sperm during puberty. (Truth)*
- *If males masturbate too much they can run out of sperm. (Lie)*

3. Going around the circle, each mother/son pair takes a turn reading their two truths and one lie. Try not to tell both of your truths first and then the lie because it makes it easier to guess.

4. Everyone in circle has an opportunity to guess which statement was the lie. Once everyone has guessed, the person will reveal what were the truths and what was the lie, and explain why the lie is false.

5. Continue around the circle until every mother/son pair has had a turn.

6. After all members have had a turn, consider the following questions as a circle:

- *Were there any statements you thought were true, but actually weren't?*

- *What is one thing you learned from this game?*

- *What could someone do who was not sure if something was a truth or a lie regarding puberty?*

Quote Study

You don't have to be afraid of change. You don't have to worry about what's being taken away. Just look to see what's been added.

Jackie Greer

....

No matter when you were born or where, puberty is the same. It's the same for your parents as it is for you – what's happening in your body dictates everything.

Francine Pascal

....

There is a young and impressionable mind out there that is hungry for information. It has latched on to an electronic tube as its main source of nourishment.

Joan Ganz Cooney

Life is change. Growth is optional. Choose wisely.

Karen Kaiser Clark

....

Pornography is the attempt to insult sex. To do dirt on it.

D.H. Lawrence

....

The first step toward change is awareness. The second step is acceptance.

Nathaniel Branden

....

One day I had to sit down with myself and decide that I loved myself no matter what my body looked like and what other people thought about my body.

Gabourey Sidibe

....

I feel like the human body is what it is, and the more you make yourself comfortable with it, the better off you are. Love your body and embrace that.

Mehcad Brooks

....

Your body is a flower that life let bloom.

Ilchi Lee

....

Men do change, and change comes like a little wind that ruffles the curtains at dawn, and it comes like the stealthy perfume of wildflowers hidden in the grass.

John Steinbeck

Control puberty? snorted the bodyguard. If you manage that, you'll be the first.

Eoin Colfer, *The Lost Colony*

....

I celebrate myself.

Walt Whitman

....

The human body is the best work of art.

Jess C. Scott

....

Heartwork

MOTHERS

1. Find a private moment to follow-up with your son about this month's circle discussion. Does he have any questions, comments, or concerns?

2. Using the recommended resources at the back of this book as a guide, purchase a book on puberty for your son. Let him know that you would love to discuss the book together when he is finished, and be sure to follow up. Or better yet, read the book together!

3. Talk with your son about pornography. Listen to his questions, concerns, and experiences, and without shaming, make your opinions and expectations known.

SONS

1. Review the notes you took in your Journey Journal during circle this month. What questions, concerns, or thoughts about puberty do you have? Share them with your mother or another trusted adult. If it feels too uncomfortable to say out loud, consider writing your message down in a note.

MONTH

11

"SEX IS SACRED"

> *It's time we saw sex as the truly sacred art that it is. A deep meditation, a holy communion and a dance with the force of creation.*
> **Marcus Allen**

Dear Mothers,

During the years of pubertal development, among the most profound changes our sons experience is the early stirrings of sexual desire. Some of our sons are beginning to explore sexual touching; they may be having their first "crush," playing "spin the bottle," attending school dances, holding hands, and more. Now arrives the season of life that children begin to discover themselves as sexual beings, and in a few short years, some of our sons will be exploring sex with a partner. Although the average age of first sexual intercourse has been rising among American teenagers, a majority of teen boys have sex at least once before finishing high school. We may wish that our sons would limit their sexual explorations to hand-holding or kissing until adulthood or marriage, but we know many teens make other choices.

As they enter the world of dating, romance, and sex, boys are often confused, ill-informed, or both. They need support for their physical and emotional well-being. It is critical for boys to be aware that if they and when they choose to have sexual intercourse, they need protection against unwanted pregnancy and sexually transmitted diseases (STDs). They also need support navigating the emotional aspects of romance and relationships, and the rules of consent and body sovereignty.

We live in a highly sexualized culture that bombards our sons with sexual messages. Our sons are going to learn about sex, so our question has to be: where do we want them to learn? They won't learn a complete truth from schools, churches, media, peers, or pornography. Our sons desperately need us to be involved in their sexual growth and development. As tempting as it may be, we must not bury our heads in the sand, ignore the complex issues of sexuality and desire, and hope it is "not an issue for my son." Sex is far too powerful and too risky for us to remain silent. When it comes to sex, what you don't know *can* hurt you. It is imperative that our sons receive correct information, in alignment with our values.

As parents, we can have a tremendous influence on our sons' sexual lives. Studies show that kids who talk to their parents about sex are more likely to delay their first sexual encounter and to practice safer sex when they do become sexually active. As our sons grow and make decisions for themselves, they will factor in the information and values we have communicated. They need our guidance here. You should know that, despite their apparent dread, kids really do want to learn about sex from their parents (this has been validated by study after study on the topic).

This month in circle, we will offer our sons holistic and comprehensive sex education, free of taboo. We will explain exactly what sex and sexual behaviors are, how to know when they are ready for sex, how take care of themselves in a sexual relationship, and how to respect the sexual rights of others. We will give our sons space to air their anxieties and questions about sex, without fear of being judged or ridiculed. We will teach our sons about the sacredness of human sexuality.

There is a lot of information to cover, but in the end, you can be assured that your son has been introduced to the most important facts you can provide on sex and sexuality. Perhaps more importantly, you will have set the stage for more discussions in the days, months, and years ahead.

"Won't this just give them ideas?"

Research shows that by having the meaningful conversations we are going to have in circle this month *by the time they are ten years old*, it becomes more likely that our sons will: postpone intercourse until adulthood, avoid impregnating someone or contracting an STD in adolescence, avoid sexually abusive relationships, and develop a healthy attitude toward sexuality. As an educator who works with elementary, middle, and high school students, and as the mother of an eighteen, thirteen, and nine-year-old, I guarantee you that our sons have already heard or will soon hear about everything we are discussing in circle this month. We are not giving them new ideas. We are teaching them how to be safe so they can enjoy a healthy sex life when the time is right, and how to discern the truth about sex from the many messages they hear elsewhere.

What will this be like?

Have you now broken into a cold sweat? Most parents feel nervous, or even terrified, talking to their children about sex. I want to reassure you that every circle I have ever held on this topic has been a success. The atmosphere is always relaxed, and the boys take it very seriously and appreciate being included in conversations about such mature and "grown up" issues. I'm sure you will feel the way one mother did when she recently remarked after one such circle, "That wasn't so bad!" and you too will be so proud of yourself.

I've found that talking about sex is like jumping into a pool of really cold water. It feels shocking and awkward for the first few minutes, but before you know it, you will become comfortably acclimated to the discussion. I promise! My advice: just jump right in and start swimming.

Final Thoughts

Given that somewhere between 5–10% of the population is homosexual, there's a chance that a boy sitting in your circle is, will be, or suspects that he might be gay. To raise sons who are tolerant of others, and so that a boy in your circle does not become confused, scared, or self-destructive if he discovers he is not heterosexual, it is vital that your language is inclusive and affirming to the wide range in which adolescent boys define and experience themselves.

Our boys are sensitive, emotional beings in all manners, including sex. Boys need space to talk about their feelings regarding sex and romance, aside from the culturally-sanctioned stereotype of the sex-obsessed teenage boy. As we established last month in our discussion on puberty, the ultimate gift we are giving our sons this month is the continued message that we are comfortable talking to them about anything on their minds. No matter what they say, we can handle it; we won't gasp in shock and we won't shame them or be ashamed of them. We are here if they are ever confused, curious, or in trouble. *We are here.*

We are in this together.

Love, *Melia*

Topic Introduction

Our Affirmation this month is: "*Sex is Sacred.*"

As we began discussing last month, one of the biggest changes of puberty is the development of sexual feelings and an increased interest in romantic relationships. You may have begun to notice that your heart flutters or you feel the sensation of butterflies in your stomach when you talk with someone to whom you feel attracted. Sexual feelings are a normal, healthy aspect of being a human. You are wired to have wonderful sexual feelings and desires, but it is important not to share those feelings with girls or boys yet.

It is our hope that one day – when the time is right – you will have a loving and satisfying sexual life, and that is why we want to talk to you about sex, love, and relationships, and answer any of your questions.

You will see, hear, and read things about sex that aren't necessarily true. You've certainly seen people kiss, date, and be sexual in movies and T.V. shows, and this month, you will learn that it is way more complicated in real life than it looks on the screen. You may have also heard about sex and sexual behaviors from your friends or other kids at school, but again, you are not likely to have received all the information you need to make the best sexual decisions for yourself.

Sex is like a coin: it has two sides. On one side, sex can be powerful, good, and life-enhancing when it occurs between two people who care about each other. Sex is how life is created! None of us would be here if it wasn't for sex! And on the other side of the coin, sex can make your life harder, it can be dangerous, and it can even be deadly. It is important that you get accurate, healthy information that is in alignment with your family's values so that you can make the right choices for yourself. This month, we are going to begin to give you that information.

About one in every ten boys is primarily attracted to other boys, others are attracted to both boys and girls, and others are primarily attracted to girls. All of the same ideas we will talk about this month in circle apply regardless of who you are attracted to.

So, what is sex?

Sex is a natural, sacred act that most adults in loving relationships find pleasurable. Essentially, in heterosexual (man and woman) sex, the man moves his erect penis in and out of the woman's vagina, and the woman moves her body with him, sometimes fast, sometimes slow. If a man's sperm cells enter into a woman's body, pregnancy can occur. A sperm cell can live for several days inside the uterus or fallopian tube. Usually a sperm cell meets a woman's egg cell in her fallopian tube. When this happens, the body of the sperm cell goes into the egg cell, the tail falls off, a protective barrier is created to not allow any other sperm in, and a baby begins to grow.

Sexual behaviors are also a part of sex. What we mean by sexual behaviors is being involved with someone else's body for the purpose of giving and receiving sexual pleasure. This includes kissing, intimate touching, oral sex, and anal sex. Oral sex is when someone puts their mouth on a woman's vulva or a man's penis, and anal sex is when a man puts his penis in someone's rectum. Although you cannot impregnate someone this way, you can contract diseases. Oral sex and anal sex are indeed, sex.

Adults also have sex for reasons other than making a baby. Sex can be fun, it can feel really good, and it can make people who already love, respect, and trust each other feel even closer. Sex is about more than the body; it is also about the heart. Sexual experiences with a loved one involve intense emotions along with physical sensations.

The two biggest risks of having sex are unplanned pregnancy and sexually transmitted diseases, also known as STDs. Teen pregnancy can happen to anyone. If your body produces sperm, and that sperm enters a woman's body, you can impregnate her. It happens. It is important to know that during sex, the penis is always leaking semen and sperm, even before ejaculation. Also, some very painful and even deadly diseases are spread through sex, such as HIV. Not everyone who has a disease knows they have it, and some people might not tell you even if they do know.

People who do not want to impregnate someone or contract a disease use protection, such as a condom. A condom is a thin rubber sheath worn on a man's penis during sexual intercourse to capture sperm so he is less likely to impregnate someone or contract a disease. The only 100% effective method to prevent pregnancy or STDs is abstinence, meaning to not have sex. For people who have sex, the next most effective method to prevent pregnancy or STDs is using a condom every time. Ultimately it is your body and you are responsible for protecting yourself.

How will you know when the time is right for you to have sex?

First of all, sex is for adults. The risks of being sexually active before you are an adult far outweigh the benefits. We firmly believe that you will have a happier and healthier life if you wait to have sex until you are an adult.

In addition to age and maturity, there are a few important qualities one must possess before engaging in sexual intercourse and sexual behaviors. Sex and sexual behaviors should only be shared with someone you love who also loves you, someone you can fully trust, and someone who respects you and whom you can respect. When it comes to sexual intercourse and sexual behaviors, these are the Big Three: *love, respect*, and *trust*. The same traits you look for in a best friend are the ones you will look for in a romantic relationship, and one day, a sexual partner. When you think about your best friend, you know that you share the Big Three, and this took time to develop, right? You didn't become best friends who love, respect, and trust each other overnight! When it comes to getting to know someone, the more time, the better. Only after months, perhaps years, of getting to know someone and sharing a significant commitment of honor and responsibility with that person will you be ready to have sex.

Please know that sex is not something you have to do to be masculine or to be a man. There are a lot of false stereotypes about boys and men regarding sex, like they always want to have sex or are always ready for it, but we know stereotypes are not true. It is your choice. Heroes never do anything before they are ready.

There is no tolerance for one person pressuring, coercing, or forcing another person into sexual behavior. If you want to do something sexual with your partner, you must hear "yes" because no one is allowed to do anything to someone's body without their permission. This is called *consent*. Consent simply means "to agree with." Sexually, consent is when both people agree about what's going to happen. ***Only "yes" means yes.*** "Maybe" doesn't mean yes and "no" absolutely never means yes. You or your partner can withdraw consent at any time, even in the middle of sex. It is okay for either person to change their mind. If this happens, everything stops. Also, it is never too late to stop being sexually active; just because you've had sex before, doesn't mean you have to keep doing it.

As we talk about romantic relationships, sexual behaviors, and sexual intercourse in circle this month, you may wish to jot down notes or questions in your Journey Journal. Please know that we, as your mothers, wish to be one of your go-to people to talk to about sex. There is nothing that you can't say to us, or ask us. We are here for you.

Discussion Prompts

1. What does a relationship built on the Big Three – love, respect, and trust – look like? What characteristics does a healthy, positive relationship have?

2. What is the difference between attraction, infatuation, and love? Is it possible to be attracted to someone who is not good for you? Why?

3. Some people feel pressured by their friends or their boyfriend or girlfriend to have sex before they are ready. What would you do if a really beautiful and very popular girl or boy wanted to have sex with you and all your friends are telling you to do it, but you don't feel ready?

4. "Sexting" is sending a text message or online post with pictures or videos of people that are provocative, naked or engaged in sex acts. Once an image is sent, it cannot be retrieved – you lose control of it. Furthermore, sexting is considered a crime for people under eighteen years of age because sexting is a form of pornography, and it is illegal for anyone to distribute child (under eighteen years old) pornography. It could get you in a lot of trouble. You should never send sexual texts, and if someone sends you a sexual text, you should delete it immediately and tell a trusted adult so they can help you with what to do next. What do you think about sexting? Why do you think people do it? How will you handle it if you are pressured or dared to send sexts?

5. Your body is *yours*. You get to determine when, how, and by whom you want to be touched, and with whom you want to be sexual. Sexual abuse is when someone is forced or persuaded to take part in sexual activities. It doesn't have to be physical contact and it can even happen online. Sexual abuse is never your fault, even if you partly wanted it or

enjoyed it. If you are ever sexually abused, it is important to tell a trusted adult so they can help you, and it is never too late to tell. Who are three trusted adults you could tell anything?

6. What does this month's Affirmation, *"Sex is Sacred,"* mean to you? In the coming month, what opportunity might you have to put this Affirmation into practice? What are some challenges you might face in practicing this month's Affirmation?

Integrated Activities

Final Checklist

Having sex is a serious responsibility. There is a lot to think about and plan for to be ready for sex. Just like a pilot must do a final checklist before take-off, this Integrated Activity represents the final checklist that you will go through before deciding to have sex.

SUPPLIES

- Blank paper – enough for each mother/son pair to have one sheet
- Pens
- Paper airplane folding instructions – these can be obtained online and printed.

INSTRUCTIONS

1. Mothers and sons pair up with one another.

2. Distribute the paper, pens, and folding instructions.

3. On one side of the paper, brainstorm a list of prerequisites, or a "final checklist," for sex. Some ideas may be: I am an adult, I love/trust/respect my partner, I have known them a long time, I want to, I have consent, I have condoms and know how to use them, no alcohol or drugs are in my body or my partner's body, etc.

4. Fold your checklist into a paper airplane and fly it!

5. Hold space for sharing and discussion among circle members.

Condom Exploration

When used correctly, condoms are an essential tool in reducing the risk of pregnancy and STDs. However, according to the most recent survey conducted by the U.S. Center for Disease Control in 2015, only 57% of sexually active teens reported condom use.

This Integrated Activity works to normalize condoms so that when our sons are eventually ready to have intercourse, they will know how to protect themselves.

SUPPLIES

* Condoms – enough for each mother/son pair to have one.

INSTRUCTIONS

1. Pass out the condoms. Each mother/son pair receives one.

2. Explain that if you want a condom to work, you have to use it correctly, and just like learning to read or playing basketball, using a condom correctly takes a certain amount of skill and practice.

3. Remind the circle that condoms should be used for oral, anal, and vaginal sex.

4. Inform the circle that condoms can be purchased at any local drugstore, and there are no age requirements for buying condoms and no prescriptions are necessary. Additionally, free condoms are available from many health clinics, sexual health agencies, and even some schools.

5. Instruct circle members to find the expiration date on their condom's wrapper. Explain that a condom should not be used past its expiration date.

6. Open your condoms. Instruct the circle to carefully tear the package at the end. Do not use your teeth or scissors, or else you could rip the condom.

7. When you open your condom's package, you will see that the condom is rolled up. The condom will only roll down one way. Discover which way your condom unrolls; the rim should be on the outside so that it looks like a little hat. Explain to the circle that if you accidently try to put a condom on inside out, you should not flip it around and use it because it will have some semen on it; you must get a new one.

8. Before a man can put on a condom, his penis must be erect. For the purposes of this Integrated Activity, use two fingers to represent an erect penis.

9. Carefully squeeze out any air in the tip of the condom before putting it on, as a trapped air bubble can cause it to tear during sex. Then roll your condom all the way down over your two fingers. Explain that when you are really using a condom, it is wise to keep the light on because sometimes a condom can rip or actually slide off and the chances are good you won't realize it because it feels virtually the same to have intercourse with or without condom. When having sex, you need to look at the condom periodically to ensure it is still on properly.

10. Demonstrate holding the condom at the base of your fingers. Explain that after the man ejaculates, he needs to hold the condom at its base against his penis as he takes his penis out of his partner's body so that no semen spills into his partner's body; this should be done before his penis gets soft, so the condom doesn't get too loose and let semen out.

11. Take the condom off, wrap the condom in tissue paper, and throw it into the garbage. Instruct the circle to never flush a condom down the toilet because it could clog the pipes and causes pollution.

12. Tell the circle that instructions for how to correctly use a condom are included in most condom boxes and can also be found online.

13. Explain that condoms cannot be reused; a new one must be used each time you have sex.

14. Hold space for questions and comments.

Quote Study

Love is friendship set on fire.

Jeremy Taylor

....

'No' is an entire sentence in itself. No means no, and when somebody says it, you need to stop.
Amitabh Bachchan

Convincing someone to have sex is the same as manipulation and does not actually count as getting consent.

Shahla Khan

....

The secret is to find someone who engages you deeply, to form a connection that goes further than desire and lust. It's not enough to covet only a face or a body, true chemistry begins with the intellect and heart.

Beau Taplin

....

Sex is essentially deep. We become what we do with our bodies, and there is no deeper act than sex.

Dietrich von Hildebrand

....

Mature love is composed and sustaining; a celebration of commitment, companionship, and trust.

H. Jackson Brown, Jr.

....

Expressions of affection, like putting your arm around someone's shoulder, holding hands, or giving a kiss goodnight, involve the principle of honesty.

John Bytheway

....

Most good relationships are built on mutual trust and respect.

Mona Sutphen

Sex lies at the root of life, and we can never learn to reverence life until we know how to understand sex.

Havelock Ellis

....

Trust is built with consistency.

Lincoln Chafee

....

Trust is the glue of life. It's the most essential ingredient in effective communication. It's the foundational principle that holds all relationships.

Stephen Covey

....

Being homosexual is no more abnormal than being left-handed.

Abhijit Naskar

....

Safe sex is an act of self-love.

Miya Yamanouchi

....

You usually have to wait for that which is worth waiting for.

Craig Bruce

Heartwork

MOTHERS

1. Talk to your son about sex, offering both information and values clarifications. Answer any questions he has, and converse with him about your expectations for his sexual behavior.

2. Human touch is proven to reduce stress, encourage self-esteem, and build community. Boys need gentle, platonic touch in their lives as much as girls do. Unfortunately, gender stereotypes extend to boys' physical expressions of touch, and in our virulently homophobic culture, all contact between men is considered suspect. As boys approach adolescence, they often pull back from hugs and other loving forms of touch, fearing it is too feminine, and many parents step back from physical contact with boys when their sons approach puberty. This leaves our sons physically isolated, only able to look to a romantic partner (a "girlfriend" or "boyfriend") for touch, where it gets blended into the sexual. This month, begin or renew your commitment to offering your son gentle, loving touch daily. Offer him hugs, high fives, foot or back massages, or a quick ruffle of his hair as you pass by. Offer to hold his hand, lean on each other, and sit beside one another. Ask him what he likes and respect his wishes.

SONS

1. What questions, thoughts, or feelings do you have from our circle discussion this month? Talk about them with your mom or another trusted adult.

2. Media can influence how we think and feel about relationships and sex by showing some things as *normal* and others as *abnormal*, or invisible. For example, movies make love seem instantaneous, portray men as preoccupied with women's bodies and sex, rarely include conversations to obtain consent, omit the use of condoms or other protection, and make sex among strangers seem like the norm. This month, notice the messages communicated in television, music, music videos, billboards, print media, and movies. What is portrayed as the norm? What information is left out or made invisible?

"I AM CHANGING
THE WORLD"

> *You cannot get through a single day without having an impact on the world around you. What you do makes a difference, and you have to decide what kind of difference you want to make.*
> **Jane Goodall**

Dear Mothers,

Every child's development of healthy self-esteem includes developing a sense of purpose and forming a habit of giving back to others. In fact, researchers have even linked a sense of purpose to lower levels of adolescent depression, less binge drinking and drug use, healthier habits such as exercising, and a greater commitment to school work.

This month, we are going to teach our sons that their lives matter, that who they are and what they do has a present and immediate impact on the world, and that the highest expression of heroism is helping those in need.

Around the age of nine, children begin to ponder the full scope of human existence and experience around the world and throughout history. Educational philosopher Rudolph Steiner called this change in consciousness the "nine-year change." According to Steiner, children at this age have questions about themselves and their purpose in the world. Many children feel shocked, sad, or even scared when they begin to confront the darker sides of our humanity: hunger, poverty, homelessness, violence, racism, sexism, pollution and climate change, war and terrorism.

Knowing that they can act to make a difference fosters a sense of control that comforts children and imbues their lives with purpose. Serving those in need teaches our sons firsthand that they have the ability to make a positive impact at any age – yes, even now! The boys will learn that they do not need to be adults, or the president of the country, to change the world, and that just by their nature they are in a position of power to make a difference. This empowering message gives our sons a sense of meaning for their lives and a confidence in their own inherent self-worth. It also reassures them that if they are ever in need, help will be available.

In classical mythology, the hero's journey always begins with a call – a call to adventure, to challenge, to service. What I want to emphasize here is that the impetus for our boys to serve is not just to fulfill needs in the community and to help others, but also to satisfy their own innate desires to live "heroic" lives rich in meaning. Our sons are destined to seek meaning in their lives through the honing of their gifts, reaching deep within, and giving something of themselves. There are many ways to make a difference, and each of us has our own unique gifts and calling. Our goal this month is to ignite a sense of purpose and passion in our sons' hearts and to amplify the native call to go forth and change the world.

We are in this together.

Love, *Melia*

Topic Introduction

Our Affirmation this month is "*I Am Changing the World.*"

Heroes are the changemakers. Heroes are the advocates, the organizers, the leaders, and the doers. Heroes show up. When heroes see something wrong in the world, they look for ways to help. Heroes make a dedicated effort of sharing their passions and talents, their time and energy, to make the world a better place. Heroes decide to notice, decide to act, and decide to make a difference. Heroes cultivate compassion in their hearts for others, and aim to practice random acts of kindness each day. Heroes ask, "what would love do?" and then they follow that path.

It is easy to get overwhelmed with the enormity and complexity of the things you would like to see done differently in the world. But remember, *all* action results in a reaction. *Everything* we do has an effect. In every moment, we can focus on doing the next right thing. We can keep it small. We can keep it simple. Our words and actions need not be big to make a difference.

There is an abundance of people and places that need help, where your time and effort can make a difference. And the really amazing thing is that helping others makes *you* feel good! You will find that knowing your value in the world and connecting with your own energy through life-affirming volunteer work gives you more purpose and direction in your life. The happiest people I've encountered all have one thing in common – they give of their time and resources to help others.

Fred Rogers, the host of the popular long-running public television children's show, *Mr. Rogers' Neighborhood*, once said, "When I was a boy and I would see scary things in the news, my mother would say to me, 'Look for the helpers. You will always find people who are helping.' To this day, especially in times of disaster, I remember my mother's words and I am always comforted by realizing that there are still so many helpers – so many caring people in this world."

In their homes, at their schools, and in their communities, heroes are the helpers. Heroes help change the world for the better.

Discussion Prompts

1. Have you ever thought about what impact you want your life to have on the world? What would you like to be known and remembered for?

2. Mother Teresa once said, "if you want to change the world, go home and love your family." What do you think she meant by that? Is it harder for you to be generous and show compassion with your family members or with strangers? Why do you think that is?

3. One of the greatest rewards of serving others is how it makes you feel about yourself. When was a time you showed someone compassion? How did it make you feel?

4. Do you recall an experience in which you were shown compassion by another person? How did that change your life? What did you learn?

5. If you could change anything in the world right now, what would it be? Which issues or causes stir the most compassion in you right now?

6. How do you or how might you use your gifts, strengths, talents, and interests to serve your community?

7. What does this month's Affirmation, *"I Am Changing the World"* mean to you? In the coming month, what opportunities will you have to put this Affirmation into practice? What are some challenges you might face in putting this Affirmation into practice?

Integrated Activity

The Tale of the Starfish

When we consider the problems of the world and the things we wish to change, it is all too easy to feel discouraged and overwhelmed and to begin asking ourselves, "how much of a difference can I really make?" When we catch ourselves thinking that way, it helps to remember *The Tale of the Starfish*.

SUPPLIES

- One typed copy of *The Tale of the Starfish* for each boy
- A starfish (these can be purchased online and at most craft stores)
- Glue sticks
- Journey Journals
- White, air-dry clay (enough for each circle member to have about two tablespoons).

INSTRUCTIONS

1. To activate the scene in their minds, ask the circle if they have ever been to the beach after a storm. Describe how after a big storm, things such as shells, ocean debris, and starfish are washed up on the shore.

2. Pass the starfish around the circle for examination and a concrete representation.

3. Read The Tale of the Starfish aloud with conviction.

The Tale of the Starfish

Adapted from "The Star Thrower", by Loren Eiseley.

Once upon a time, there was an old man who used to go to the ocean to do his writing. He had a habit of walking on the beach every morning before he began his work. Early one morning, he was walking along the shore after a big storm had passed and he found the vast beach littered with starfish as far as the eye could see, stretching in both directions.

Off in the distance, the old man noticed a small boy approaching. As the boy walked, he paused every so often and as he grew closer, the man could see that he was occasionally bending down to pick up an object and throw it into the sea. The boy came closer still and the man called out, "Good morning! May I ask what it is that you are doing?"

The young boy paused, looked up, and replied, "Throwing starfish into the ocean. The tide has washed them up onto the beach and they can't return to the sea by themselves. When the sun gets high, they will die, unless I throw them back into the water."

The old man replied, "But there must be tens of thousands of starfish on this beach.

I'm afraid you won't really be able to make much of a difference."

The boy bent down, picked up yet another starfish and threw it as far as he could into the ocean. Then he turned, smiled and said, "It made a difference to that one!"

4. After the facilitator has read the story aloud, pass the talking stick around the circle to invite responses.

   • *What feelings did you have hearing this story?*

   • *What do you think is the moral of the story?*

   • *How might you relate this story to your own life?*

5. Each circle member glues a copy of *The Tale of the Starfish* into their Journey Journal.

6. To serve as a concrete reminder of our Affirmation this month and of the lessons gleaned in *The Tale of the Starfish*, each circle member molds their piece of white air-dry clay into the shape of a starfish.

DIRECTIONS

1. Knead the clay until it is soft.

2. Roll the clay into a ball in the palm of your hands.

3. Divide the clay into five equal parts.

4. Roll each part into five thick elongated sections. These are the legs.

5. On parchment paper, draw five lines meeting at a center point.

6. Place the sections on the lines. Overlap the ends meeting at the center point and pinch them together. This becomes the middle body/mouth of the starfish.

7. Wet your fingers in water and smooth out the junction of pieces in the middle. Run a wet finger along the legs as well.

8. Let it dry for 1 minute.

9. Use skewers to create a more realistic, textured effect by poking holes on the star fish.

10. Let it dry and harden completely.

11. Place the starfish on your home Hero's Heart altar as a reminder of the powerful moral in *The Tale of the Starfish*.

The Ripple Effect

The inspiring concept of the ripple effect is based on the understanding that we are all connected and therefore the choices we make, both big and small, impact not only ourselves but also the world around us. Thoughts, words, and actions are like stones dropped in a pond and they create ripples that travel outward. Everything we do, think, and say affects the people in our lives and their reactions in turn affect others.

SUPPLIES

- One large bowl of water
- One small pebble for each circle member.

INSTRUCTIONS

1. Place a bowl of water on the central altar space.

2. Pass out the pebbles – one for each circle member.

3. Explain to the circle that the pebble represents you, your life, and your choices. The water represents the people around you – your family, friends, peers, school, community, planet.

4. Demonstrate how when we (hold up a pebble) live with the heart of a hero and practice kindness, such as smiling at someone, offering an encouraging word or a helping hand – we create ripples that spread to affect others (drop pebble in the water) far beyond the initial act.

5. One at a time, each circle member shares one example of an act of kindness or service they have done or will do, and then gently drops their pebble in the water, watching as the ripples symbolize the far-reaching effects that one act can have.

6. Remove the pebbles from the water and dry them off. Each circle member takes their pebble home as a reminder of the sacred power we each have to change the world, one small act at a time.

Quote Study

Life's most urgent question is, what are you doing for others?

Dr. Martin Luther King, Jr.

....

Do all the good you can, by all the means you can, in all the ways you can, in all the places you can, at all the times you can, to all the people you can, as long as you ever can.

John Wesley

....

You change the world by being yourself.

Yoko Ono

....

Yesterday I was clever, so I wanted to change the world. Today I am wise, so I am changing myself.

Rumi

....

Each time a man stands up for an ideal, or acts to improve the lot of others, or strikes out against injustice, he sends forth a tiny ripple of hope, and crossing each other from a million different centers of energy and daring, those ripples build a current that can sweep down the mightiest walls of oppression and resistance.

Robert Kennedy

....

Your work is to discover your work, and then with all your heart to give yourself to it.

Buddha

A tree is known by its fruit; a man by his deeds. A good deed is never lost; he who sows courtesy reaps friendship, and he who plants kindness gathers love.

Saint Basil

....

Too often we underestimate the power of a touch, a smile, a kind word, a listening ear, an honest compliment, or the smallest act of caring, all of which have the potential to turn a life around.

Leo Buscaglia

....

There is a vitality, a life force, an energy, a quickening, that is translated through you into action, and because there is only one of you in all time, this expression is unique, and if you block it, it will never exist through any other medium; and be lost. The world will not have it.

Martha Graham

....

Never worry about numbers. Help one person at a time, and always start with the person nearest you.

Mother Teresa

....

The best portion of a good man's life is his little nameless, unremembered acts of kindness and of love.

William Wordsworth

....

Do not let what you cannot do interfere with what you can do.

John Wooden

Every action of our lives touches on some chord that will vibrate in eternity.

Edwin Hubbell Chapin

....

I don't know what your destiny will be, but one thing I know: the only ones among you who will be really happy are those who have sought and found how to serve.

Dr. Albert Schweitzer

Heartwork

MOTHERS AND SONS

Choose a service project to complete together this month. Volunteering together helps forge a stronger bond between the two of you, empowers your son, and helps communities – all at the same time! It's a win-win-win! You may wish to spend an afternoon volunteering at the local food pantry or animal shelter, picking up litter off the street, helping an elderly neighbor with yardwork, or collecting items to donate to the local homeless shelter. Follow your son's passions and interests, and help him to channel his energy for the greater good. The options are limitless!

CLOSING CIRCLE AND
RITE OF PASSAGE CEREMONY:
"I AM CROSSING THE THRESHOLD"

Dear Mothers,

Congratulations! You and your son have completed a powerful twelve-month journey together! Your Hero's Heart circle shared a life-changing experience that will always be remembered and cherished. The purpose of this closing circle is to mark and honor the circle's completion in a special way, and to provide a space for reflection and closure. The ceremony portion serves to bring focus and intention to the moment, engaging the sacredness of the experience and acknowledging your son's gradual transition into manhood.

This month's culminating circle will take form with some preparation from all circle participants. Discussing in advance the flow of the closing circle and ceremony will facilitate an understanding among everyone, and preparing some items will ensure a fitting experience for a powerful conclusion.

Depending on where your circle has been gathering, you may wish to relocate for the rite of passage ceremony. A change of scene can be just the thing to dedicate the final experience. The location you choose for the ceremony should feel special – perhaps a place with sentimental associations or a beautiful locale in nature. The original Hero's Heart circles always enjoyed an overnight mother-son campout at a scenic lake-side campground for the closing circle and ceremony. We have found it most potent to transition immediately from the closing circle into the rite of passage ceremony, followed by a cheerful celebration with s'mores and fellowship around the campfire. However, you may consider holding the closing circle on a separate date and time from the rite of passage ceremony and celebration. I encourage you to practice sovereignty as a circle of mothers, deciding what format would be the most meaningful for your sons and easeful for you.

We are in this together.

Love, Melia

Topic Introduction

Our Affirmation for this closing circle and ceremony is "*I Am Crossing the Threshold.*"

To open the circle this month, speak about your initial intentions for starting the circle, some of the themes and activities the group explored, moments and qualities of the group that stood out for you, and the importance of the closing circle and ceremony.

Discussion Prompts

1. What are three important things you learned this year?

2. What topics or activities meant the most to you?

3. How have you developed or changed as a person over the course of our Hero's Heart year?

4. Who in our circle has helped, inspired, or influenced you this year? In what ways?

5. What is something we did this year that you will remember for the rest of your life?

6. What gifts did you receive from our circle this year and how will you take them with you out into the world?

7. What does our Affirmation, "*I Am Crossing a Threshold,*" mean to you?

Quote Study

(This month's quote study will require thought and preparation ahead of time.)

Over the course of the year together, your circle has explored many powerful quotes that capture the values heroes hold true. For this month's quote activity, each circle member will share a personal "life motto." A motto is a guiding principle or expression that a person strives to live by every day, like a personal mission statement. It is basically a concise statement of beliefs or ideals that may either be a sentence or a short phrase. A life motto serves as a reminder of larger lessons taught and serves as a guide post and verbal beacon along the roads we travel. It helps us find our bearings and stay on course. My personal life motto is "love matters most." When I am faced with a decision, remembering my motto helps me choose the path of love (for self, for others, for life) over fear. Some other examples of life mottos are:

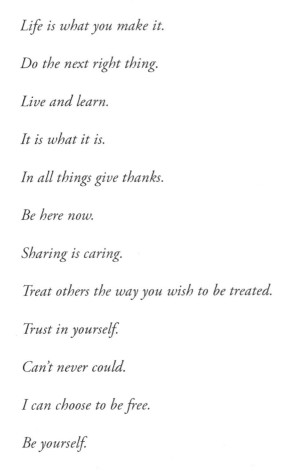

Life is what you make it.

Do the next right thing.

Live and learn.

It is what it is.

In all things give thanks.

Be here now.

Sharing is caring.

Treat others the way you wish to be treated.

Trust in yourself.

Can't never could.

I can choose to be free.

Be yourself.

Your motto might be inspired by a favorite quote from previous Quote Studies or another quote you love, or one you completely create and write yourself.

Three questions will help create your own life motto:

- *What are my core values?*
- *What values do I most want to be known and remembered for?*
- *What values will most improve the person I am today?*

Each circle member will create and record their personal life motto in their Journey Journal ahead of time. In circle, each participant will share their personal life motto and what it means to them. As you speak your motto aloud in circle, and each time thereafter, let the words sink down inside and become part of the essence of who you are and how you seek to live.

Write down each person's motto in quotations with their name under it in your Journey Journals.

Integrated Activity

Sacred Giveaway

The Sacred Giveaway is a ritual I first learned from a wise elder in my community, Christy Gray. It is essentially the practice of giving away useful and even beloved possessions to others. Not with the thought of having 'strings attached' to the gift, or having regrets from having given the gift, but to sacrifice something important to ourselves in order to allow for personal growth and to connect deeply with others.

SUPPLIES

Each participant brings a gift from their world that has been meaningful in some way and reflects the growth journey they have experienced in circle this year. This is not a gift to be purchased, but rather something you already have and feel is time for another person to own. I have seen rocks, feathers, clothing, paintings, books, candles, baseball cards, art, household items, decorations and even a telescope brought as sacred gifts. What counts is not the monetary value of the item, but rather the intention behind the gift and what it represents.

INSTRUCTIONS

Have each person place their unwrapped gift on the center altar. Then decide who will go first (we usually like to keep the selection random by picking a number between one and twenty or drawing straws with one cut short). Whoever is chosen to go first then goes to the altar and chooses the gift that calls to them. They will say, "I believe this is my gift" and share why they chose it. They then ask, "Who brought me this gift?" At that point, the person who brought the gift will tell the story of the object and what it represents to them. For example, a boy in a past circle chose to bring his favorite Rubik's Cube as his Sacred Giveaway item to symbolize how over the course of the year he had learned to meet challenges head on. It is then the giver's turn to receive a gift from the altar. And so it goes until all the gifts are given and each person has a special reminder of the magic that was shared together that year.

Rite of Passage Ceremony

A rite of passage ceremony marks the transition of one phase of life to another, in this case, the transition from boyhood to adolescence. The Hero's Heart rite of passage ceremony provides space for the community to transmit its core values and confer to the young initiates the responsibility of living with the "heart of a hero."

SUPPLIES AND PREPARATION

- Smudge stick to energetically clear the space. Palo Santo and White Sage are my favorites!

- One large candle to place in the center of the ceremonial circle.

- Create a beautiful threshold on the ground to demarcate the boys' ceremonial entrance into the circle using natural items such as flower petals, pebbles, pinecones, shells, rocks, sticks, driftwood, etc.

- Small taper candles and drip protectors – one for each circle member.

- In the Native American tradition, medicine bags were meant to give guidance, good fortune, good health, protection, abundance, and even love to the individuals who carry them. For the ceremony, we respectfully borrow this sacred tradition with gratitude to our Native American brothers and sisters. Purchase one leather drawstring medicine pouch with strings long enough to wear around the neck safely for each boy. These can be purchased online, ideally from a Native American store: support Native artists!

- Each mother should select and bring small items for each boy to represent a spiritual gift or value she would like to bestow upon him to carry into his future. Some ideas are: sage, sweetgrass, cedar, beans, seeds, flowers, leaves, feathers, shells, gemstones, crystals, rocks, buttons, beads, charms, coins, and keys. A mother may choose to give the same item to each boy, or unique items can be chosen for each boy. Prior to the ceremony, each mother should determine the word or phrase that the item symbolizes.

- Our ancestors' lives and legacies have contributed to our existence today, and by honoring them we honor a timeless part of ourselves. During the ritual, the boys will each have an opportunity to call in their ancestral line by name. In preparation, each boy should prepare to recite the first names of his parents (or step-parents or anyone with an active role in raising him) and all of his grandparents.

- Invite the boys to dress in the same color shirt, or alternatively, in formal attire.

1. Prepare the space for ceremony by smudging the land or room to symbolically clear any energy that doesn't belong.

2. Place and light the large white candle at the center of the ceremony space.

3. As you've done at the beginning of circle each month, ceremoniously smudge each of the boys while singing the chorus of "Meditation on Breathing" by Sarah Dan Jones. An audio recording of the song can be obtained online at **https://tinyurl.com/ydx6em88**

When I breathe in, I breathe in Peace

When I breathe out, I breathe out Love.

When I breathe in, I breathe in Peace

When I breathe out, I breathe out Love.

[Repeat.]

BODY

1. The mothers will take their places, standing evenly-spaced in a half-circle. The sons will stand just beyond the threshold at the mouth of the circle opening.

2. The boy to go first will meet his mother at the threshold and pause.

3. His mother will ask him this sacred question, loud enough for all to hear: "Son, who are you?"

4. At this time, the son will call in his ancestral line and claim his status as Hero. For example, "I am Erick James, son of Melia and Rick, grandson of Rosemary, John, Sandy, Jim, and Friedbert, and I have the heart of a hero."

5. The boy's mother will lovingly place his medicine pouch around his neck and speak to him briefly about her unconditional love, gratitude, and pride for him. She will then return to her place in the circle.

6. The boy, wearing his empty medicine pouch around his neck, will travel the circle, stopping at each mother. When the boy comes to a circle mother, she will place the item she brought for him in his medicine pouch and speak the words "On your hero's journey,

may you always be/have/remember ___." Mothers may feel called to offer a hug or loving embrace to the boy, respectful of consent and comfort level, of course. The boy will then move to the next mother.

7. Once he has made his way around the half-circle of mothers, he will take his place standing with his own mother as the next boy approaches the threshold and takes his turn.

8. Continue in this way until all the boys have had the opportunity to be recognized, honored, and given their gifts.

CLOSING

1. Pass out the small white taper candles with drip protectors.

2. As you have closed circle each month, close the ceremony by together singing "The Light Within" by John Kramer.

3. The facilitator will light her candle from the large white candle burning in the center of the circle. She will then turn to light the candle of the person standing beside her, who will then turn to light the candle of the next person, all the way around the circle. Repeat the song until all the candles are lit.

4. In unison, recite the closing benediction and blow out your candles.

5. Celebrate with food, photographs, and togetherness! Your circle has shared an experience that you will remember for the rest of your lives!

PARTING WORDS

When they ask how far love goes, when my job's done, you'll be the one who knows.
Dar Williams

Dear Mothers,

The adolescent years can be a hard time for our sons to go through, and it can prove to be an especially challenging season for us as mothers. In watching my own sons grow, I have found that this time of life is like walking a tightrope bookended by two towering platforms: childhood and young adulthood. The precarious path that our sons must walk to grow up and become the men they are meant to be is exhilarating. It is also scary as hell.

We don't know exactly what unique obstacles and challenges lie ahead of our sons. What we *do* know is that he needs a soft place to land. *As much as our sons crave freedom, they crave security.* The effort you put in to creating an intentional, loving community of other mothers and sons will build a safety net for your son. A place to center himself on his values. A place that, when he falls, will offer him the support he will need to dig deep and get back up.

There is an old saying that "the ones who see the light must carry the torch." It is my deepest hope that in reading this book, your eyes have been fully opened to the needs and capacities of your beloved son, and that I have succeeded in illuminating a path forward for you to send your boy into the world as a hero. I hope that my words have left you feeling inspired to start your own Hero's Heart circle and that you will carry the torch into your community and improve the way we raise our boys.

Trying to end sexism by bringing about gender equality is a daunting objective. After all, each of us is only one person, one mother. However, just as we taught our sons in Month 12, we must not allow the overwhelm of what we cannot do prevent us from doing what we can. As mothers, we have tremendous power to influence our sons' perspectives, and like envisioning ripples on a pond, we can only imagine just how far our influence might extend. The time is now to nurture the sacred masculine in our culture, and by extension, to celebrate manhood as a co-creator to the greater good for all. Each of us can have a hand in making our society healthier and strong for all. We must not underestimate our power, dear mothers, for it will be from the ongoing and enduring acts of our maternal love that a new day will dawn.

We are in this together.

Love, *Melia*

RESOURCES

Much of what I have written in this book comes from my experience as an educator, circle facilitator, and mother of boys. I have also made much use of scientific research and other scholarly work. The resources listed below are selected books and research articles that have influenced my thinking and this book.

Books

The Adolescent Psyche: Jungian and Winnicottian Perspectives, by Richard Frankel

The Child's Changing Consciousness, Eight Lectures, by Rudolf Steiner

The Forty-Nine Percent Majority: The Male Sex Role, by Deborah David and Robert Brannon

Masculinity Reconstructed: Changing the Rules of Manhood – At Work, in Relationships, and in Family Life, by Ronald F. Levant

The Will to Change: Men, Masculinity, and Love, by bell hooks

Manhood in America, by Michael Kimmel, PhD

Guyland: The Perilous World Where Boys Become Men, by Michael Kimmel, PhD

The Wonder of Boys, by Michael Gurian

Real Boys: Rescuing Our Sons from the Myths of Boyhood, by William Pollack

Oedipus Wrecks: How Mothers Are Pushed Away From Their Sons and Why They Should Push Back, by Kate Lombardi

The Courage to Raise Good Men: You Don't Have to Sever the Bond with Your Son to Help Him Become a Man, by Olga Silverstein and Beth Rashbaum

Strong Mothers, Strong Sons Raising the Next Generation of Men, by Ann F. Caron

Boys Will Be Men: Raising Our Sons for Courage, Caring, and Community, by Paul Kivel

It's a Boy!: Your Son's Development From Birth to Age 18, by Michael Thompson and Teresa Barker

The War Against Boys: How Misguided Policies Are Harming Our Young Men, by Christina Hoff Sommers

A Fine Young Man: What Parents, Mentors, and Educators Can Do to Shape Adolescent Boys into Exceptional Men, by Michael Gurian

The Male Experience, by James A. Doyle

Hold on to Your Kids: Why Parents Need to Matter More Than Peers, by Gordon Neufeld

Of Woman Born: Motherhood as Experience and Institution, by Adrienne Rich

Calling the Circle: The First and Future Culture, by Christina Baldwin

The Different Drum: Community Making and Peace, by Scott Peck

The Men from the Boys: Rites of Passage in Male America, by Ray Raphael

From Boys to Men, by Bret Stephenson

The Art of Ritual: Creating and Performing Ceremonies for Growth and Change, by Renee Beck and Sydney Barbara Metrick

Rituals of Manhood, by Gilbert Herdt

The Hero with a Thousand Faces, by Joseph Campbell

Trauma-Proofing Your Kids: A Parents' Guide for Instilling Confidence, Joy, and Resilience, by Peter A. Levine, PhD and Maggie Kline

Protecting the Gift: Keeping Children and Teenagers Safe (And Parents Sane), by Gavin De Becker

Positivity, by Barbara Fredrickson

Delusions of Gender, by Cordelia Fine

Packaging Boyhood: Saving Our Sons from Superheroes, Slackers and Other Media Stereotypes, by Lyn Mikel Brown, Sharon Lamb and Michael Tappan

Raising Cain: Protecting the Emotional Life of Boys, by Michael Thompson

Deep Secrets: Boys' Friendships and the Crisis of Connection, by Niobe Way

The Friendship Factor: Helping Our Children Navigate Their Social Worlds – and Why It Matters for Their Success and Happiness, by Kenneth H. Rubin

The Buddy System: Understanding Male Friendship, by Geoffrey L. Grief

Best Friends, Worst Enemies: Understanding the Social Lives of Children, by Michael Thompson, Catherine O'Neill-Grace and Lawrence Cohen

Masterminds & Wingmen: Helping Our Boys Cope with Schoolyard Power, Locker-Room Tests, Girlfriends, and the New Rules of Boy World, by Rosalind Wiseman

Lost Boys: Why Our Sons Turn Violent and How We Can Save Them, by James Garbarino, PhD

Sticks and Stones: Defeating the Culture of Bullying and Rediscovering the Power of Character and Empathy, by Emily Bazelon

Boys Will Be Boys: Breaking the Link Between Masculinity and Violence, by Myriam Miedzian

Nonviolent Communication: A Language of Life, by Marshall B. Rosenburg PhD and Deepak Chopra

The Achilles Effect: What Pop Culture is Teaching Young Boys about Masculinity, by Crystal Smith

Emotional Intelligence, by Daniel Goleman

The Adonis Complex: How to Identify, Treat, and Prevent Body Obsession in Men and Boys, by Harrison Pope

What Your Child Needs to Know About Sex (And When): A Straight-Talking Guide for Parents, by Dr. Fred Kaeser

For Goodness Sex: Changing the Way We Talk to Teens about Sexuality, Values, and Health, by Al Vernacchio

The Purpose of Boys: Helping Our Sons Find Meaning, Significance, and Direction in Their Lives, by Michael Gurian

The Path to Purpose: How Young People Find Their Calling in Life, by William Damon, PhD

The Purpose Driven Life, by Rick Warren

A New Earth: Awakening to Your Life's Purpose, by Eckhart Tolle

Articles

Amin, A., Kågesten, A., Adebayo, E., Chandra-Mouli, V. (2018) 'Addressing gender socialization and masculinity norms among adolescent boys: policy and programmatic implications.' *The Journal of Adolescent Health*, 62, S3–S5.

Westwood, M., Pinzon, J. (2008) 'Adolescent male health.' *Pediatrics & Child Health,* 13, 31–36.

Levant, R. F., Allen, P. A., Lien, M-C. (2014) 'Alexithymia in men: how and when does the deficit in the processing of emotions occur?' *Psychology of Men and Masculinity*, 15, 324-334.

Rogers A.A., Updegraff K.A., Santos C.E., Martin C.L. (2017) 'Masculinity and school adjustment in middle school.' *Psychology of Men and Masculinity,* 18, 50-61.

Kornienko O., Santos C.E., Martin C.L., Granger K.L. (2016) 'Peer influence on gender identity development in adolescence.' *Developmental Psychology,* 52, 1578-1592.

Gupta T., Way N., McGill R.K., Hughes D., Santos C., Jia Y., Yoshikawa H., Deng H. (2013) 'Gender-Typed Behaviors in Friendships and Well-Being: A Cross-Cultural Study of Chinese and American Boys.' *Journal of Research on Adolescence*, 23, 57-68.

Barker G., Ricardo C., Nascimento M., Olukoya A., Santos C. (2010) 'Questioning gender norms with men to improve health outcomes: Evidence of impact.' *Global Public Health*, 5, 539-553.

Galdas, P., & Cheater, F., Marshall, P. (2005) 'Men and health help-seeking behaviour: Literature review.' *Journal of Advanced Nursing*, 49, 616-23.

Hicks, S. (2008) 'Gender role models... .who needs 'em?' *Qualitative Social Work*, 7, 43-59.

Bricheno, P., Thornton, M. (2007) 'Role model, hero or champion? Children's views concerning role models.' *Educational Research*, 49, 383-396.

Carbonell, D., Reinherz, H., Giaconia, R. (2002) 'Adolescent protective factors promoting resilience in young adults at risk for depression.' *Child and Adolescent Social Work Journal*, 19, 393.

Weir, K. (2017) 'Maximizing children's resilience.' *American Psychological Association*, 48, 40.

Johnson, K., Caskey, M., Rand, K., Tucker, R. Vohr, B. (2014) 'Gender differences in adult-infant communication in the first months of life.' *American Academy of Pediatrics*, 134, 6.

Mascaro, J., Hackett, P., Rentscher, K., Mehl, M. (2017) 'Child gender influences paternal behavior, language, and brain function.' *Behavioral Neuroscience*, 131, 262-273.

Erdley, C., Newman, E., Carpenter, E. (2001) 'Children's friendship experiences and psychological adjustment: theory and research.' *New Directions for Child and Adolescent Development*, 2001, 5-24.

McPherson, M., Smith-Lovin, L., & Brashears, M. (2006) 'Social isolation in America: changes in core discussion networks over two decades.' *American Sociological Review*, 71, 353-375.

Reif, A., Freitag, C., Schneider, M., Eujen, A., (2007) 'Nature and nurture predispose to violent behavior: serotonergic genes and adverse childhood environment.' *Neuropsychopharmacology*, 32, 2375–2383.

'Beyond Male Role Models: gender identities and work with young men.' An Open University research project working with Action for Children Funded by the Economic and Social Research Council. http://www.open.ac.uk/health-and-social-care/research/beyond-male-role-models/report

If your son wishes to go deeper, the following books and websites will support his Hero's Heart journey each month.

Month 1

Heroes for My Son, by Brad Meltzer

Stories for Boys Who Dare to Be Different: True Tales of Amazing Boys Who Changed the World Without Killing Dragons, by Ben Brooks and Quinton Wintor

The Book of Awesome Women: Boundary Breakers, Freedom Fighters, Sheroes, and Female Firsts, by Becca Anderson

What Do You Stand For?: A Guide to Building Character, by Barbara Lewis

Month 2

The Struggle to be Strong: True Stories by Teens Overcoming Tough Times, by Al Desetta and Sybil Wolin

Who Moved My Cheese? For Teens, by Spencer Johnson

Conquering Negative Thinking for Teens, by Mary Alvord and Anne McGrath

Month 3

Gender Identity, by Cynthia Winfield

The Psychology of Sex and Gender, by Jennifer Bosson, Joseph Vandello, and Camille Buckner

We Should All Be Feminists, by Chimamanda Ngozi Adichie

Month 4

Don't Let Your Emotions Run Your Life for Teens, by Sheri Van Dijk

A Still Quiet Place for Teens, by Amy Saltzman

Emotions!: Making Sense of Your Feelings, by Mary Lamia

Month 5

A Good Friend: How to Make One, How To Be One, by Ron Herron and Val J. Peter

Communication Skills for Teens: How to Listen, Express, and Connect for Success, by Michelle Skeen and Matthew McKay

A Teen's Guide to the 5 Love Languages: How to Understand Yourself and Improve All Your Relationships, by Gary Chapman

Month 6

How to Say No and Keep Your Friends: Peer Pressure Reversal for Teens and Preteens, by Sharon Scott

Stick Up for Yourself: Every Kid's Guide to Personal Power & Positive Self-Esteem, by Gershen Kaufman

The Courage to Be Yourself: True Stories by Teens about Cliques, Conflicts, and Overcoming Peer Pressure, by Al Desetta

Month 7

Making it Right: Building Peace, Settling Conflict, by Marilee Peters

The Kids' Guide to Working Out Conflicts: How to Keep Cool, Stay Safe, and Get Along, by Naomi Drew

Month 8

Body Language, Intuition, and Leadership, by Orly Katz

Mindfulness Meditations for Teens, by Bodhipaksa

Month 9

A Kid's Guide to Drugs and Alcohol, by Chance Parker

Messages About Me: Wade's Story: A Boy's Quest for Healthy Body Image, by Educate and Empower Kids

Indigo Teen Dreams, by Lori Lite

Month 10

What's Happening to My Body? Book for Boys, by Lynda Madaras and Simon Sullivan

What's Going on Down There? A Boy's Guide to Growing Up, by Karen Gravelle

Guy Stuff: The Body Book for Boys, by Cara Natterson

The Body Book for Boys, by Rebecca Paley and Johnathan Mar

Good Pictures, Bad Pictures: Porn Proofing Today's Young Kids, by Kristen Jensen and Gail Poyner

Month 11

Dating and Sex: A Guide for the 21st Century Teen Boy, by Andrew P. Smiler, PhD

It's Perfectly Normal: Changing Bodies, Growing Up, Sex, and Sexual Health, by Robie Harris

Free Your Mind: The Book for Gay, Lesbian, and Bisexual Youth and Their Allies,
by Kate Kaufman and Ellen Bass

Month 12

Breakthrough: How One Teen Innovator is Changing the World, by Jack Andraka

It's Your World: Get Informed, Get Inspired, and Get Going!, by Chelsea Clinton

The Teen Guide to Global Action: How to Connect with Others (Near & Far) to Create Social Change,
by Barbara Lewis

ABOUT THE AUTHOR

Melia Keeton-Digby is an author, circle facilitator, and speech-language pathologist specializing in dyslexia. She is the founder and creator of The Nest, a sacred gathering space in Georgia, USA, where she leads mother-daughter and mother-son empowerment circles. She is passionate about supporting mothers in raising confident and connected children. Her first book, *The Heroines Club: A Mother-Daughter Empowerment Circle*, has seeded circles around the US, UK, Europe and beyond. Melia lives in Watkinsville, Georgia with her husband and three children, ages eighteen, thirteen, and nine.

Through her books, Melia provides mothers with a revolutionary model for empowering their daughters, nurturing their sons, and strengthening the mother-child relationship. *The Heroines Club* and *The Hero's Heart* are more than just books; they are a movement.

She is available for speaking engagements, guest facilitation, and coaching.

meliakeetondigby.com

SELECTED TITLES
FROM WOMANCRAFT PUBLISHING

The Heroines Club: A Mother-Daughter Empowerment Circle

MELIA KEETON-DIGBY

Nourishing guidance and a creative approach for mothers and daughters, aged 7+, to learn and grow together through the study of women's history. Each month focuses on a different heroine, featuring athletes, inventors, artists, and revolutionaries from around the world – including Frida Kahlo, Rosalind Franklin, Amelia Earhart, Anne Frank, Maya Angelou and Malala Yousafzai as strong role models for young girls to learn about, look up to, and be inspired by.

In a culture that can make mothering daughters seem intimidating and isolating, it offers an antidote: a revolutionary model for empowering your daughter and strengthening your mother-daughter relationship.

The Heroines Club is truly a must-have book for mothers who wish to foster a deeper connection with their daughters. As mothers, we are our daughter's first teacher, role model, and wise counsel. This book should be in every woman's hands, and passed down from generation to generation.

Wendy Cook, founder of Mighty Girl Art

Reaching for the Moon: a girl's guide to her cycles

LUCY H. PEARCE

The girls' version of Lucy H. Pearce's Amazon bestselling book *Moon Time*. For girls aged 9–14, as they anticipate and experience their body's changes, *Reaching for the Moon* is a nurturing celebration of a girl's transformation to womanhood.

A message of wonder, empowerment, magic and beauty in the shared secrets of our femininity … written to encourage girls to embrace their transition to womanhood in a knowledgeable, supported, loving way.

thelovingparent.com

The Goddess in You

PATRÍCIA LEMOS & ANA AFONSO

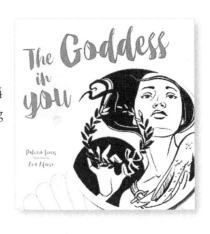

The Goddess in You is especially created for girls aged 9-14 years, offering a unique, interactive approach to establishing cycle awareness, positive health and well-being.

- 13 double-sided cycle mandalas illustrated with goddesses

- Instructions for use

- An introduction to the 13 featured Greek goddesses

- A basic, age-appropriate introduction to the menstrual cycle

- Self-care tips for health and well-being

A simple and beautiful invitation to help girls build a relationship with their menstrual cycle. We highly recommend this book for all young menstruating women.

Alexandra Pope & Sjanie Hugo Wurlitzer, co-authors of *Wild Power*

WOMANCRAFT PUBLISHING

Womancraft Publishing was founded on the revolutionary vision that women and words can change the world. We act as midwife to transformational women's words that have the power to challenge, inspire, heal and speak to the silenced aspects of ourselves.

We believe that:

- books are a fabulous way of transmitting powerful transformation,

- values should be juicy actions, lived out,

- ethical business is a key way to contribute to conscious change.

At the heart of our Womancraft philosophy is fairness and integrity. Creatives and women have always been underpaid. Not on our watch! We split royalties 50:50 with our authors. We work on a full circle model of giving and receiving: reaching backwards, supporting Tree-Sisters' reforestation projects, and forwards via Worldreader, providing books at no-cost to education projects for girls and women.

We are proud that Womancraft is walking its talk and engaging so many women each year via our books and online. Join the revolution! Sign up to the mailing list at womancraftpublishing.com and find us on social media for exclusive offers:

(f) womancraftpublishing

(y) womancraftbooks

(o) womancraft_publishing

womancraftpublishing.com

Made in the USA
Monee, IL
17 August 2020